USS *Arizona*

The Enduring Legacy
of a Battleship

Ingo W. Bauernfeind

BAUERNFEIND
PRESS

Dedication

This book is dedicated to those sailors and Marines—both living and dead—who served on board the battleship USS *Arizona*, those who gave their lives on December 7, 1941 and during the following years of fighting, until the bloodiest war in history ended.

    It is dedicated also to my family, in particular to my mother, Mrs. Heidi Bauernfeind, for her endless support, encouragement, and trust in all my endeavors—without her this book would never have been possible.

How to watch the three videos in this book (pages 66, 124, 139):

1. Open your mobile app store (App Store, Google Play, Windows Marketplace, etc.)
2. Search for free QR code readers.
3. Simply download the QR code reader to your smartphone or tablet, open it and you are ready to go.
4. Open the QR code reader on your device.
5. Hold your device over a QR code so that it's clearly visible within your screen. Two things can happen when you correctly hold your device over a QR code:
   - The phone automatically scans the code.
   - On some readers, you have to press a button to snap a picture, not unlike the button on your smartphone camera.
6. If necessary, press the button. Your smartphone reads the code and navigates to the intended video website, which doesn't happen instantly. It may take a few seconds on most devices.
7. Watch the video by after selecting the correct resolution (up to 4K).

ISBN: 978 3 98159 842 1

1st Edition / Copyright © 2018

Bauernfeind Press
Hingbergstrasse 86-88
45468 Mülheim an der Ruhr
Germany
Email: email@ingobauernfeind.com
www.ingobauernfeind.com
www.bauernfeindpress.com

Layout by WS WerbeService Linke, Alberichstr. 11, 76185 Karlsruhe, Germany
Cover design by WS Werbeservice Linke
Printed in Slovenia through Gorenjski Tisk Storitve, 4000 Kranj

Content

ACKNOWLEDGEMENTS

First of all, I want to express my deepest gratitude to my friend and mentor, historian Daniel A. Martinez; the survivors of the USS *Arizona*; and the U.S. National Park Service. During my college education at Hawaii Pacific University in Honolulu I completed an internship at the USS *Arizona* Memorial (now the World War II Valor in the Pacific National Monument). With naval history and Pearl Harbor being life-long passions for me, I felt honored to work with this renowned institution. During my cooperation with Daniel Martinez over the years, my connection to him grew constantly. Despite his commitments as a noted historian, Daniel always supported my ambitions with his expertise and advice.

My personal contact to the survivors of the *Arizona* encouraged me to preserve their memories for the future. I want to thank each of them for sharing their intimate thoughts and feelings with me: Donald G. Stratton, the late Glenn H. Lane, the late Edward L. Wentzlaff, and the late John D. Anderson. I also want to express my gratitude to the late Zenji Abe, his daughter Naomi Shin, Sterling R. Cale, and Charlie Van Valkenburgh. Abe was a Japanese pilot who participated in the attack on Pearl Harbor. After the war, he dedicated his energy to the reconciliation between the United States and Japan. Abe very kindly contributed an essay about his motivation to reconcile with his former enemies. Mr. Cale is a Pearl Harbor survivor who was assigned to remove the human remains from the *Arizona's* wreck. He graciously allowed me to include his personal experience in this book. Charles Van Valkenburgh, the grandson of the *Arizona's* last commanding officer, Franklin Van Valkenburgh, kindly shared his thoughts about his grandfather. The National Park Service (NPS) and the Pacific Historic Parks are the stewards of the USS *Arizona* Memorial and the World War II Valor in the Pacific National Monument. I want to thank the people at these institutions for their support: Tom Shaw, Kay English, Skip Wheeler, Jennifer Burbank, Ray Sandla, Joey Hutton, and many others.

The Submerged Resources Center (SRC) of the National Park Service, based in Denver, Colorado, has been monitoring, surveying, and photographing the remains of the *Arizona* since the 1980s. The SRC staff has provided me a fascinating insight into the ship as an archaeological site and environmental challenge for the future, for which I am endlessly grateful: Brett T. Seymour (with Steve Burns and Jorge Franzini at Curiosity Stream for giving me permission to include their photography and film about the *Arizona* in my book), Daniel J. Lenihan, Dr. David L. Conlin, Matthew A. Russell, Larry E. Murphy, and Evan Kovacs.

I also want to thank the following individuals and institutions for their support: Marcus Linke, Joyce Libby, Paul Stillwell, Michael W. Pocock, Burl Burlingame, William J. Blackmore, Dr. James P. Delgado, Janis Jorgensen and Captain Tim Woolridge (USN, ret.) at the U.S. Naval Institute, Paul Wentzlaff (Edward L. Wentzlaff' son), Garth and Trish Anderson (Trish is the daughter of Glenn H. Lane), Nikki Stratton (Donald G. Stratton's granddaughter), Honolulu Star Bulletin, Josef Kaiser, Judith Bowman at the U.S. Army Museum Hawaii, David Rush (U.S. Navy), Heather Postema, Bolling Smith at the Coast Defense Study Group, Inc., Maury Drummond and Tim NesSmith at the USS Kidd Veterans, Dr. Geoffrey White, Ernest Arroyo, Mark Nitta, Bonnie Beatson, Lisa O'Brien, Sebastian Boll, Dr. Maximilian Dorndorf, Johanna Langer, Jochen Lehmann, Dr. Werner Haas, the late Kris Smith, Joe Kane (U.S. Navy), Glen L. Bower, Karl Backman, Klaus Hagedorn, Lutz Strenger, Philip and Cyril Coombes, Jessica Sims at the John F. Kennedy Presidential Library and Museum, Hawaii State Archives, U.S. National Archives, U.S. Naval Historical Center, National Geographic Society, U.S. Navy/Pearl Harbor Station Hawaii, U.S. Department of Defense, and U.S. Library of Congress.

FOREWORD
The Enduring Legacy of a Battleship

Naval or maritime archaeologists often refer to shipwrecks as time capsules. After their descent to a watery grave, once proud ships often remain undisturbed on the sea bottom for decades, centuries or even forever with time having stopped on board. If discovered and explored, shipwrecks open a door into the past, thus becoming valuable for archaeological research or even treasure hunting. But is this really everything? What remains beyond a deteriorating hull in the depths of the ocean? Long before I moved to Honolulu I had been captivated by the history of the Hawaiian Islands, the Pacific, and the story of Pearl Harbor in particular. Over the years I have visited the USS *Arizona* Memorial numerous times beginning to think about the sunken battleship as a time capsule–the *Arizona* took her place in history when she settled on the bottom of Pearl Harbor on December 7, 1941.

Marking the greatest loss of life on a single ship in U.S. Naval history, she is a tomb and memorial for the 1,177 men who perished with her. Although large portions of her superstructure, masts, and gun turrets have been removed and scrapped, the ship's interior has remained widely undisturbed since the end of the salvaging operations in 1943. The hulk has become a war grave for more than 900 sailors and Marines still resting inside her.

During my visits to Pearl Harbor, I often wondered what would remain of this once proud ship and its crew for the future? Physical remains, survivor accounts, photos, artifacts, and souvenir items? While trying to find an answer to this question I got the inspiration to write this book. It is important to me to show that the *Arizona* and her legacy live on in various ways–even in form of a radio-controlled ship model.

A tour of the memorial usually ends with the visitors leaning over the railing to get a glimpse of the rusting hulk below them. With this book I want to invite the reader–who has probably visited the memorial–to go on a journey that begins where the tour of the memorial ends–with a dive into history. Diving down to the *Arizona* is a special and emotional experience–during the dive we are only a few inches of steel away from the grave of more than 900 men who died long before their time. Civilians are not allowed to dive the wreck site–the *Arizona* is in general accessible only to National Park Service personnel. This makes the circle of individuals with the privilege of this unique experience very small. Therefore, firsthand accounts from the members of the NPS Submerged Resources Center provide an insight into what it means to explore the *Arizona*. Moreover, I wanted to present a laudable portrait of the ship and her crew. I had the honor of meeting several *Arizona* survivors and was fortunate to interview some of them. These oral histories will bring the ship alive– the survivors talk about ship life, friends, how they experienced the *Arizona's* sinking and how this affected their lives.

This book includes three films about the *Arizona* which can be accessed and viewed by using the QR-code scanner of a tablet or cell phone. Produced by the SRC and Curiosity Stream, the three films provide survivor stories, the science of stewardship and an interior survey of the *Arizona*.

Reading about the survivors' memories is one thing–watching them on a TV screen is an even more emotional experience. Their personal accounts and connections to their ship, their former comrades, and the memorial in Pearl Harbor are the key part of this book– when I listened to them talking about the *Arizona*, I could see in their eyes, how their ship came to life again.

Personal essays, written by the survivors, the grandson of the ship's last captain, historians, and even by a former enemy, give the reader an understanding of what the *Arizona* and her legacy means to them. In addition to the interviews the film features spectacular underwater footage of the sunken *Arizona* narrated by Brett Seymour, the former chief of the National Park Service's Submerged Resources Center.

This book is not a recollection of the ship's history from launch to destruction. The noted historian and author Paul Stillwell has captured the *Arizona's* life in his wonderful book *Battleship Arizona–An Illustrated History* (U.S. Naval Institute Press), which I highly recommend as the standard work on the subject. History should always be a lesson for the future, in particular when it is told by eyewitnesses who experienced and sacrificed more than many of us can imagine.

If this work can make a contribution to the preservation of the *Arizona's* legacy for the future, this would be the greatest reward for me.

Ingo Bauernfeind

Mülheim, Germany
November 2018

INTRODUCTION

By Daniel A. Martinez

Nearly eight decades have passed since the guns fell silent in Europe and in the Pacific. The hatred and the brutality of World War II have been tempered by time, but the memory and the monuments, speak to us in a variety of voices. For the young, it is a part of history that has been passed on by the grandparents or the sons and daughters. The monuments dot the landscape of Europe and the Pacific. But for Americans, there is one monument to one ship and to one crew that will never be surpassed in the memory of World War II for that nation.

In 1962, the U.S. Congress saw the completion of a federal memorial at Pearl Harbor. The USS *Arizona*, a ship that suffered the greatest loss of life of any warship in the nation's history, was formally remembered by the placement of a white spanning memorial that stretched across the width of the sunken battleship. On Memorial Day, formal commemorative activities were held to christen the USS *Arizona* Memorial. For most Americans, it is the most famous World War II event, primarily because it was our entry into World War II and one of America's darkest defeats.

The way Americans remember Pearl Harbor has evolved since World War II. During the war years "Remember Pearl Harbor" became the battle cry of our nation. It galvanized the country against the enemies of the United States. It not only propelled us into the war in the Pacific but, strangely, this slogan translated itself to the struggle in Europe. Pearl Harbor became the symbol for America's entry into World War II.

In 1945, the nation and the world were exhausted by the struggle. As peace settled in, the need for a time of remembrance and a desire to commemorate Pearl Harbor slowly evolved among the American people. It took twenty-one years for a formal memorial to be built. It would take several decades more for a national day of commemoration to be established.

But Pearl Harbor has gone beyond its formal remembrance. It is now an iconic moment in American and world history. The term "Remember Pearl Harbor" has taken on a different meaning. Books, magazines, and newspapers continually carry stories about the people and the events of December 7, 1941. Popular films and television programs recapture those moments.

Pearl Harbor now provides an opportunity for reflection. We look back and watch the World War II generation fade slowly away. We wonder what lessons we have learned, and we stand in awe of those of the "Greatest Generation". Over the years, some profound stories have been shared with the National Park Service and its rangers. On an autumn day, an elderly woman approached a park ranger and said: "This memorial, to me, is a place of hope." Puzzled, the ranger replied: "Madam, I have heard a number of descriptions from people about the Memorial but not one has mentioned hope. May I ask why you have used that reference?" She replied: "Well, young man, I was a young woman held in a camp called Auschwitz and when we heard that the United States was now in the war, it gave us hope that we might survive." She then extended her arm and revealed a tattoo on her arm as if to verify the truth that she had spoken. At that moment, a new reference point for the Memorial was established.

But the Memorial has different meanings for different people. The Pearl Harbor Survivors Association, men and women who survived the attack of December 7, 1941 on Oahu, see the Memorial as a place in which a message should be invoked to all who visit. That message is to keep America alert and to remember Pearl Harbor. Some of the *Arizona* survivors believe that the oil that still seeps from the ship is not only a message of the sacrifice of that crew, but they also believe that when the oil stops flowing, the last survivor of the *Arizona* will have passed. But it's not just the veterans who comment on the Memorial's lessons and power, it's also prominent visitors. Madeline Albright, former Secretary of State, stated as she stared down at the skeletal remains of the ship: "How sad. How very sad."

For Tom Brokaw, it is the feeling that the Memorial is a place that defined modern America and galvanized a nation to propel itself to victory through a unification of a generation that had collaborative goals and single purpose.

As Dame Elizabeth Taylor looked at the wall, she was overcome with the enormity of the loss and the knowledge that her country of birth, Great Britain, had struggled for two years prior to Pearl Harbor. They felt that with the Americans at their side, victory, which seemed so distant, was now possible.

But just as the interpretation of Pearl Harbor and its Memorial changes and evolves, so have the facilities that interpret the attack through its exhibits and new historical interpretation. In 2010 an extensive renovation was done with the construction a new 50-million-dollar visitor center providing fresh opportunities both in the area of comfort and interpretive learning. A new educational center is part of this complex. It affords students and teachers an opportunity to learn about the attack on Pearl Harbor and the Pacific War. This connective museum complex tells the story of America and Japan and their perilous journey down the road to Pearl Harbor. Museum artifacts, audio-visual applications, and interactive exhibits are intended to personalize an understanding of Pearl Harbor and the tragic outbreak of the Pacific War, thus bringing the war in Europe and the war in the Pacific to a global consequence... World War II.

At the center of Pearl Harbor experience is a 23-minute documentary film that sets the mood and understanding for the visitors' eventual trip by boat to the Memorial. This tactile visit to the USS *Arizo*-

na Memorial is the core experience for all visitors and gives them the opportunity, not only to experience history, but also to actually touch it and it, in turn, it is hoped, touches them.

Pearl Harbor, at present, has become what Alfred Preis, the architect of the USS *Arizona* Memorial, always believed it should be... a place where former enemies can meet in peace to remember a time of war. Now the passage of time has depleted the ranks of those who witnessed or participated in the drama of December, 7 1941. The children of those veterans and their grandchildren now inherit this history and in doing so, pause each December 7th not only to commemorate that tragic day but also to appreciate the value of the peace that has existed between America and Japan since 1945. Certainly the monumental official visit on December 27, 2016 of President Obama and Prime Minister Abe to the USS *Arizona* Memorial was historically significant. It brought these two leaders together for that final official gesture of reconciliation between the two countries that had clashed in such a bitter war. In that way, both nations remember and honor their common bond of history and now celebrate seventy years of peace between them.

Daniel A. Martinez,
Chief Historian
WWII Valor in the Pacific
National Monument
Pearl Harbor, November 2018

Biography

Daniel A. Martinez is a noted historian. He has lectured on a wide variety of historical topics and has written and published many articles on Pearl Harbor, the Pacific War, and American history. Mr. Martinez has co-authored a new book, *Kimmel and Short and Pearl Harbor* (U.S. Naval Institute Press 2005) and presented papers at prestigious gatherings such as the Organization of American Historians, the IPMS National Convention in Atlanta (2005) and Phoenix (2006), the National Council on Public History, the Western History Association, and the Oral History Association. Currently, Mr. Martinez is an adjunct professor at the Naval War College in Newport, Rhode Island.

Daniel Martinez has appeared as a camera personality on programs for ABC, NBC, CBS, and CNN, the History Channel, the Discovery Channel, the Learning Channel, the Military Channel, the National Geographic Channel, the Travel Channel, and ZDF (Germany). Currently, he is the host and historian-in-residence for "Unsolved History" on the Discovery Channel. He has served in the National Park Service since 1979.

The bugle that was aboard the battleship USS *Arizona* on December 7, 1941 rests on the American flag as a reminder of that fateful day at Pearl Harbor.
[U.S. Department of Defense]

LIFE OF THE BATTLE-SHIP USS *ARIZONA*

1916 – 1941

Assistant Secretary of the Navy Franklin Delano Roosevelt (fourth from left) attends the keel laying ceremony for the new battleship *Arizona* at the New York Navy Yard on March 16, 1914. During his presidency, the United States would enter World War II after the Japanese attack on Pearl Harbor in December 1941.
[USS *Arizona* Memorial Photo Collection, USAR-652]

Lowering of the first keel plate into place March 16, 1914. The Brooklyn Bridge is in the background.
[USAR-653]

The *Arizona's* stern surrounded by a framework of scaffolding, April 1915.
[U.S. Library of Congress]

The construction of the battleship USS *Arizona* (BB-39), named for the 48th state in the Union, began on March 16, 1914 when the keel was laid. After a year of intense labor she was launched on June 19, 1915 as the second and last of the *Pennsylvania*-class battleships. The launching was a grand affair. Esther Ross, daughter of an influential pioneer citizen in Prescott, Arizona, was selected to christen the ship. The battleship's commissioning took place on October 16, 1916 under the command of Captain John D. McDonald. The dimensions of the ship were quite impressive for the time. Her overall length was 608 feet (two American football fields long) with a beam of 97 feet. She displaced 35,852 tons (full load) with a mean draft of 29 feet. Four Parsons turbines and twelve Babcock & Wilcox boilers developing 34,000 horsepower drove the *Arizona's* four shafts. She could reach a top speed of 21 knots. The designated complement was 1,087 men in 1916. She was well armed for battleships of her time. The original armament during World War I consisted of twelve 14-inch guns, twenty-two 5-inch guns, four 3-inch antiaircraft guns, and two 21-inch submerged torpedo tubes. She was protected by 18 inches of armor at her maximum thickness. The *Arizona* and her sister ship, *Pennsylvania*, represented a modest improvement of the previous *Nevada*-class battleships. Length and displacement were some-

what increased, two 14-inch guns were added, and the main armament refitted with four triple-gun turrets. The most significant change was concentrated in the vessel's firepower. The *Arizona's* four turrets (labeled No. 1, 2, 3 and 4) each mounted three 14-inch naval guns.

In November 1916, the *Arizona* departed on her shakedown cruise and training off the Virginia Capes, Newport and Guantanamo Bay, Cuba. Two months later she returned to Norfolk, Virginia to conduct test firing of her guns and perform torpedo defense exercises. In December she entered the New York Naval Shipyard for a post-shakedown overhaul that was completed in April 1917. While in New York, the *Arizona* received

orders to join Battleship Division 8 at Norfolk, Virginia, which was to be her homeport through World War I while she served as a gunnery-training vessel. Due to the scarcity of fuel oil in the European theater, the *Arizona*, an oil burner, stayed home in American waters to patrol the East Coast. When the armistice was signed she sailed for Portsmouth, England to operate with the British Grand Fleet. A month later the new battleship was ordered to rendezvous with the transport *George Washington* that was carrying President Woodrow Wilson to the Paris Peace Conference. President Wilson carried a bold proposal intended to ensure a lasting world peace. In his outline for world cooperation, Wilson proposed 14 points to act as guidelines for a peace without victory, and a new world body called the League of Nations. The *Arizona* would act as honor escort for the voyage to Brest, France.

In June 1919, the *Arizona* entered the New York Naval Shipyard for maintenance and remained there until January 1920, when she departed for fleet maneuvers in the Caribbean. That summer, the *Arizona* became the flagship for Battleship Division 7, commanded by Rear Admiral Eberle, the future chief of naval operations. The *Arizona* continued operations in the Caribbean Sea throughout the winter, and during that period made her first passage through the Panama Canal. The ship returned to Norfolk from Cuba in April 1921, and was overhauled in the New York Navy Yard. That summer, the *Arizona* participated in experimental bombing exercises by seaplanes on a captured German U-boat, the first in a series of joint Army-Navy experiments conducted during June and July of 1921 to measure the effectiveness of air attacks. On July 1, 1921, the *Arizona* was honored as the flagship for three-star Vice Admiral John D. McDonald. McDonald had served as the ship's first commanding officer. With the flag came the title of flagship of the Battle Force, U.S. Atlantic Fleet. In August, the flag was transferred to the battleship *Wyoming* and the *Arizona* received a new

admiral, John S. McKean, commander of Battleship Division 7. In September of 1921, the *Arizona* was transferred to Pacific waters. At San Pedro, California, she underwent another change of command, when Rear Admiral Charles Hughes became the new commander of Battleship Division 7. For the next decade the *Arizona* served as flagship for Battleship Divisions 2, 3, and 4. A number of distinguished officers served aboard the vessel, particularly Rear Admirals William V. Pratt and Claude Block. During this period the ship sailed twice to Hawaii to participate in fleet maneuvers and practice amphibious landings of Marines. In February 1929, the *Arizona* passed through the Panama Canal for fleet maneuvers in the Caribbean. On May 1, the battleship returned to Norfolk in preparation for a modernization overhaul. On May 4, 1929, she entered the Norfolk Navy Yard for that purpose and was placed in reduced commission. During this modernization stage the *Arizona* received a massive facelift. First to go were the traditional cage masts that were replaced fore and aft by tripod types. New 5-inch antiaircraft guns replaced the outdated 3-inch mounts. New armor was added below the upper decks to guard against the fall of shot by high-angle gunfire and bombs dropped by aircraft. Extra compartments called "blisters" were added to the outer

hull to increase the ship's protection against torpedo attack. In an effort to offset the additional weight, a new power plant consisting of modern boilers and turbines was installed to allow it to maintain normal fleet speed. The engines were upgraded with new-geared units, and the original boilers were replaced with six Bureau Express three-drum boilers. The *Arizona's* fuel capacity was increased from 2,332 to 4,630 tons of oil. On March 1, 1931,

modernization was completed, and the *Arizona* was placed in full commission once again.

One of the more significant events in the ship's history took place on March 19, 1931, when President Herbert Hoover and his party embarked the *Arizona* for a 10-day inspection cruise to Puerto Rico and St. Thomas in the Virgin Islands; they were then transported to Hampton Roads at month's end. The *Arizona* left Nor-

The completed bow section.
[U.S. National Archives]

To Christen Super-Dreadnought

ESTER ROSS

Prescott, Ariz., May 1.—To Miss Ester Ross, native of Arizona and daughter of the city of Prescott, will go the honor of christening the battleship Arizona when that monster of the deep slides from the ways in the Brooklyn navy yard on June 19. The appointment of Miss Ross was announced by Governor Hunt. Miss Ross is a typical representative of Arizona's younger generation of women. She was seventeen years old on November 9, 1914, and has lived all her life in Prescott. A committee of fifty leading citizens from all parts of Arizona has been appointed by Governor Hunt to attend the launching and a special train will run from Phoenix to New York.

The launching was a grand affair, and Esther Ross, daughter of an influential pioneer citizen in Prescott, Arizona, was selected to christen the ship.
[USS *Arizona* Memorial Photo Collection]

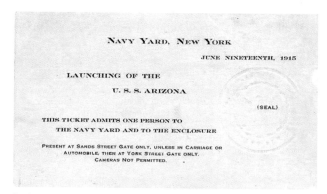

Invitation to the *Arizona's* launching ceremony on June 19, 1915.
[USS *Arizona* Memorial Photo Collection]

Miss Esther Ross (right) holds the christening bottles and halyard. The man behind her is Mr. George Hunt, the Governor of Arizona.
[Courtesy of Paul Stillwell / U.S. Navy Photograph]

Arrival of the official delegation from Arizona for the launch of the new battleship.
[U.S. National Archives]

Miss Esther Ross christens the *Arizona*.
[U.S. National Archives]

folk for the last time on August 1, 1931, and remained in the Pacific for the rest of her operational life. Rear Admiral Chester Nimitz hoisted his flag as commander of Battleship Division 1 on September 17, 1938, with the *Arizona* serving as his flagship until May 1939. His successor, Rear Admiral Russell Willson, assumed command in San Pedro, California. As tensions grew in the Pacific, so did fleet responsibilities. On April 2, 1940, the *Arizona* moved into Hawaiian waters, but was ordered to the west coast to be overhauled at Puget Sound Naval Shipyard in Washington. The work was completed by January 23, 1941. At that time Rear Admiral Isaac C. Kidd relieved Rear Admiral Willson and took command of Battleship Division 1. The *Arizona* returned to Hawaii in February 1941, and trained in those waters for four months. The last voyage to the West Coast occurred in June, and in early July the battleship returned to Pearl Harbor. For several months prior to the outbreak of the Pacific War, the *Arizona's* crew underwent intensive battle-readiness drills that often included mock air attacks from the carrier *Enterprise*. The battleship entered dry dock No. 1 on October 27, 1941, for minor adjustments and re-

The new battleship afloat after its launch.
[U.S. National Archives]

A large crowd watches as the *Arizona* slides into the East River.
[USAR-809]

pairs. Soon after, the *Arizona* rejoined the fleet. The ship's exact movements for the month before the Pearl Harbor attack are not clear, as the ship's log was lost in the sinking. She entered Pearl Harbor on December 6, 1941, and moored on the east side of Ford Island. The repair ship *Vestal* pulled alongside to ready the vessel for repair work scheduled for the following Monday. At 10:00 a.m. that morning, Admiral Kidd came aboard the *Vestal* for a 15-minute official call. Later, the captain of the repair ship, Cassin Young, boarded the *Arizona* to discuss the ship's pending repairs with the battleship's chief engineer. Many of the ship's crew had liberty that Saturday. Some of the married men had wives on the island and received weekend passes. However, a majority of the men had returned to the ship by midnight. Eight hours later the *Arizona* would be lying on the bottom of Pearl Harbor with the bodies of most of those men.

Tugboats move the *Arizona* to the pier where she will be completed.
[USAR-62]

The new battleship is moored alongside a pier in the New York Navy Yard on its commissioning day on October 17, 1916.
[U.S. Library of Congress, LC-B2-4026-5]

Rear Admiral Nathaniel R. Usher and Captain John
D. McDonald (right), *Arizona's* first commanding
officer, on board the battleship on the day of its
commissioning.
[U.S. Library of Congress, LC-B2-4026-10]

The *Arizona* steams in formation with other Atlantic
Fleet battleships, during gunnery practice, circa
1917. After the United States entered the war, she
spent most of her time as a gunnery training ship in
the Chesapeake Bay.
[Courtesy of Paul Stillwell / Naval Historical Center,
NH 95244]

The *Arizona* goes up the
East River to Tempkinsville,
New York, following sea tri-
als on December 24, 1916.
[USAR-50]

Stern view, port side of the *Arizona* in 1917.
[U.S. Library of Congress, 19-LC-19A-22]

The *Arizona* in Guantanamo Bay, Cuba, January 1, 1920. This photo was taken after the first modernization, which included the raising of the searchlight platforms and the installation of control stations for the secondary guns on the two cage masts.
[USAR-661]

The *Arizona* during a great naval review after the end of World War I at New York City on December 26, 1918.
[U.S. Navy, HD-SN-99-02136]

If you had been on the Arizona

HERE she comes, homeward bound, with "a bone in her teeth," and a record for looking into many strange ports in six short months.

If you had been one of her proud sailors you would have left New York City in *January*, been at Guantanamo, Cuba, in *February*, gone ashore at Port of Spain, Trinidad, in *March* and stopped at Brest, France, in *April* to bring the President home. In *May* the Arizona swung at her anchor in the harbor of Smyrna, Turkey. In *June* she rested under the shadow of Gibraltar and in *July* she was back in New York harbor.

Her crew boasts that no millionaire tourist ever globe-trotted like this. There was one period of four weeks in which the crew saw the coasts of North America, South America, Europe, Asia and Africa.

An enlistment in the navy

gives you a chance at the education of travel. Your mind is quickened by contact with new people, new places, new ways of doing things.

Pay begins the day you join. On board ship a man is always learning. There is work to be done and he is taught to do it well. Trade schools develop skill, industry and business ability. Work and play are planned by experts. Thirty days furlough each year with full pay. The food is fine. A full outfit of clothing is provided free. Promotion is unlimited for men of brains. You can enlist for two years and come out broader, stronger, abler. "The Navy made a man of me" is an expression often heard.

Apply at any recruiting station if you are over 17. There you will get full information. If you can't find the recruiting station, ask your Postmaster. He knows.

Shove off! — Join the U. S. Navy

Stern view of the *Arizona* in one of the Panama Canal locks, 1921. The canal connects the Atlantic with the Pacific.
[Courtesy of Paul Stillwell / U.S. Library of Congress]

Left side: Recruiting advertisement in 1919.
The U.S. Navy had to rebuild its personnel
strength after countless men had left the
service after the end of World War I.
[Courtesy of Paul Stillwell / Alfred C. Holden
Collection]

The battleship's bow photographed from the bridge during the passage through the canal.
[USAR-1791]

This aerial view of the *Arizona* was taken from a kite balloon.
[Courtesy of Paul Stillwell / Joseph C. Driscoll Collection]

The *Arizona* steams through the canal, 1921.
[U.S. Naval Historical Center, NH 101676]

The *Arizona* at anchor in Caribbean waters, early 1920s. The casemates had been closed after the guns' removal.
[USAR-677]

The *Arizona's* catapult with the Nieuport airplane. Note the cage mast in the background. [U.S. Naval Institute Photo Collection]

A French Nieuport airplane on the catapult atop gun turret No. 3. [U.S. National Museum of Naval Aviation, 1996.253.7217.003]

An aerial photograph of the *Arizona* at anchor. The 1920s saw the advent of air power. U.S. Army Air Service pilots under the command of Billy Mitchell bombed and sank the captured German battleship SMS *Ostfriesland*. This demonstrated the effectiveness of aerial bombardment on warships. The results of this and other tests indicated what might happen to battleships in the future, when attacked from the air. At that time, nobody could anticipate what might happen to the *Arizona* and the other warships in Pearl Harbor two decades later. The modern aircraft, launched from an aircraft carrier, soon would eclipse the age of the battleship and become a decisive weapon in all theaters of World War II.
[USAR-681]

Aerial view of the *Arizona* leading a the battle fleet during maneuvers in the Atlantic.
[USAR-660]

Crew inspection on board the *Arizona*.
[U.S. Naval Institute]

Captain Harlan P. Perrill commanded the *Arizona* from
June 1925 to May 1927.
[USS *Arizona* Memorial]

Captain Ward K. Wortman commanded the ship from September 1928 to April 1930. The *Arizona* had twenty-five
commanding officers between 1916 and 1941.
[Courtesy of Paul Stillwell / Nellie Main Collection, *Arizona*
Reunion Association]

Civilian visitors aboard the *Arizona* in front of gun turret No. 4 in San Francisco, 1923. The battleship carried twelve 14-inch guns in four triple gun turrets. The maximum range of the main artillery was nearly 20 miles.
[USAR-35]

The *Arizona* fires a salvo during target practice, 1920s.
[U.S. Naval Historical Center, NH 78118]

The 14-inch guns of the *Arizona* originally had a range range of 23,000 yards which increased to more than 30,000 yards after modernization.
[Courtesy of Paul Stillwell]

Drawing of the *Arizona* firing a broadside.
[U.S. Naval Historical Center, NH 83970]

This photograph of the *Arizona's* port side shows the 5-inch casemate guns and the rear side of the second 14-inch gun turret. The number of 5-inch guns was eventually reduced from twenty-two to twelve.
[USAR-688]

Projectiles splash close to
the *Arizona* during target
practice.
[USAR-1773]

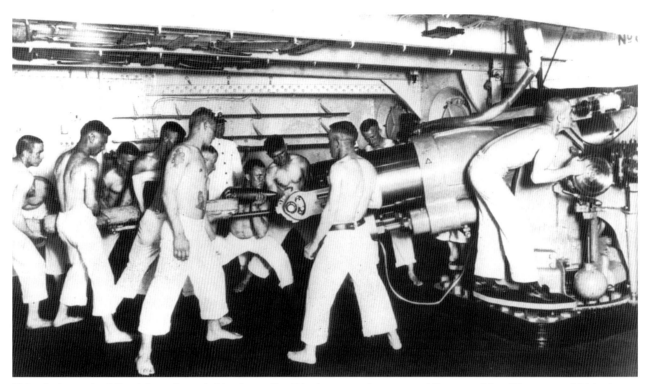

This photograph of the *Arizona's* port side shows the 5-inch casemate guns and the rear side of the second 14-inch gun turret. The number of 5-inch guns was eventually reduced from twenty-two to twelve.
[USAR-688]

Crew members use a dolly to move a torpedo on deck.
[USAR-844]

The crew stands by to load the 3-inch antiaircraft gun.
[USAR-750]

The Atlantic Fleet steaming up New York Harbor on its return from winter maneuvers in the West Indies, May 1920. This photograph was taken from the battleship Pennsylvania with her sister ship *Arizona* in front of her. A seaplane flies overhead.

[U.S. Naval Historical Center, NH 69012]

The *Arizona* in dry dock, early 1920s. Note the torpedo tube below the waterline markings which was used to attack enemy surface ships.
[USAR-02]

Right side: *Arizona's* stern in dry dock, 1921. Men scrap and paint the hull protecting it from corrosion.
[USAR-666]

The *Arizona* during a naval review, 1927. The "E" on the smokestack stands for excellence and indicates outstanding performance of the ship's crew.
[U.S. National Archives, 19-LC-19C]

Close-up ot the "E" on the ship's smokestack.
[USAR-689]

The *Arizona* passes the Statue of Liberty, 1920s.
[Courtesy of Paul Stillwell]

Race-boat teams compete for a trophy during the 1920's. This competion was very prestigous among sailors from various battleships. The *Arizona* is at anchor in the background. Her race-boat won on that day.
[USAR-688]

The *Arizona's* race-boat team poses with trophy.
[Courtesy of Paul Stillwell, Earl Phares Collection]

The *Arizona* during the early stage of her modernization at the Norfolk Navy Yard, 1929.
[U.S. Naval Historical Center, UA 473.01]

The *Arizona* has almost completed her modernization, December 1930. Major changes included thicker horizontal armor, larger fuel capacity, heavier antiaircraft guns, and increased torpedo protection.
[Norfolk News Service Photo Courtesy of Ernest Arroyo, Pearl Harbor Associates via Paul Stillwell]

Left side: The construction of a new foretop on the tripod mast, 1929. The new tripod masts were strong enough to support three-level fire control tops for the main and secondary batteries.
[Courtesy of Paul Stillwell / USS *Arizona* Memorial Photo Collection, USAR-1800]

Starboard view of the modernized *Arizona*. Note the new 5-inch antiaircraft guns on the 02-level. When the Japanese attacked Pearl Harbor in 1941, the ship's antiaircraft armament was obsolete.
[U.S. Library of Congress, 19-LC-19B-4]

The new tripod mast with the modified bridge.
[USAR-1802]

Left: Close-up of the modernized bridge and foretop.
[USAR-1801]

The *Arizona's* bow hits a wave. American battleships like her were notoriously "wet" ships, much to the discomfort of her crews.
[USAR-1781.01]

The *Arizona* in dry dock in Pearl Harbor. Her name could be found at the stern but not at the bow.
[USAR-793]

The *Arizona* goes though rough seas, 1930s. After her modernization, the *Arizona* had a displacement of 37,654 tons (full load).
[U.S. Naval Historical Center, NH 671]

The *Arizona* could reach a top speed of 21.23 knots and had a range of 13,600 nautical miles at a speed of 15 knots. [USAR-691]

With President Herbert Hoover on board, *Arizona* returns from a cruise to the West Indies, 29 March 1931.
[U.S. Naval Historical Center, NH 93550]

Aerial view of the *Arizona* in dry dock No. 1 at the Pearl
Harbor Navy Yard, March 1932.
[USAR-58]

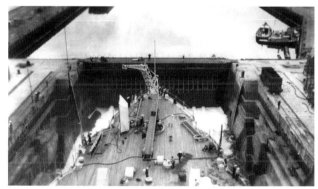

The stern section of the *Arizona* in dry dock. Note the
catapult and crane.
[USAR-685]

Right: View of the bow from the bridge.
[USS *Arizona* Memorial Photo Collection, USAR-1783.04]

The *Arizona* in dry dock, 1934. The men work on stages to scrap marine growth from the bottom before it can dry and harden.
[U.S. Naval Institute]

Bow view of the *Arizona* in dry dock. Note the torpedo blisters on both sides, which were installed to protect the hull against torpedoes from submarines, destroyers, and airplanes.
[USAR-7921]

Two crew members pose in front of a 5-inch deck gun.
[USAR-1796.01]
Right: The *Arizona's* baseball team in 1937.
[U.S. Naval Institute]

The *Arizona* at sea with three floatplanes on catapults.
[U.S. Naval Historical Center, 80-G-1021397]

Bedding hangs out to dry. The open hatch in the foreground provides ventilation for the compartments below. [USAR-818]

A metal locker with the personal belongings of a crew member. Note the book with the cover titled *Mein Kampf*, known as Adolf Hitler's autobiography. [USAR-646]

Crew members in the *Arizona's* galley pose for a photograph. They had to prepare meals for more than 1,700 men every day. [USAR-41]

Two crew members at the mess table. Note the stowed hammocks in the background. For most of the enlisted men on board the *Arizona*, their bed was a hammock. [USAR-752]

A sailor prepares a refreshment in the ship's galley.
[USAR-648]

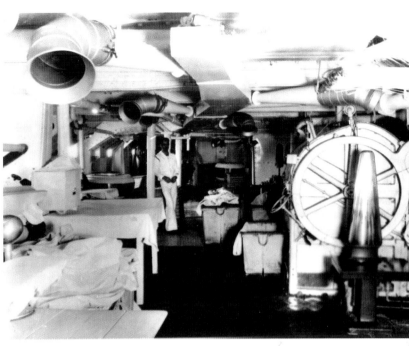

The laundry room aboard the battleship *Arizona*.
[USAR-648]

One of Arizona's two ship bells. One is preserved at the
USS *Arizona* Memorial, the other one at the University of
Arizona, Tucson.
[USAR-693]

Crew member M. C. Matthews poses in his sweater in
front of one of the 5-inch deck guns. He belonged to the
Arizona's race-boat team.
[USAR-70]

Arizona's band at Pearl Harbor's Bloch Arena on November 26, 1941. All members of the band died during the Japanese attack on December 7, 1941.
[USAR-55]

Two Vought-Sikorsky OS2U floatplanes on the *Arizona's* stern in 1939.
[USAR-836]

The *Arizona* during fleet maneuvers astern of the battleships *Tennessee* and *Texas* (in lead).
[U.S. Naval Institute]

Left side: The launch
of a seaplane from the
catapult.
[USAR-73]

The ship's crane lifts one of the float-
planes, probably a Curtiss SOC Seagull,
back on the ship.
[Courtesy of Michael W. Pocock / U.S. Navy
Photograph]

Right: The *Arizona's* float-planes are on deck, one ready for catapult launching.
[U.S. Naval Historical Center, NH 93552]

Below: This is one of the last known portrait photographs of the *Arizona* before her destruction. The battleship *Nevada* is in the background. The picture was taken on January 18, 1941.
[Courtesy of Michael W. Pocock / Puget Sound Naval Shipyard]

DECEMBER 7, 1941
Death of the *Arizona*

*The attack affected all of us... In my
case it was the loss of my twin brother–
both of us were on the USS Arizona.*

– John D. Anderson

The *Arizona* ablaze, immediately following
the explosion of her forward magazines.
[USAR-364]

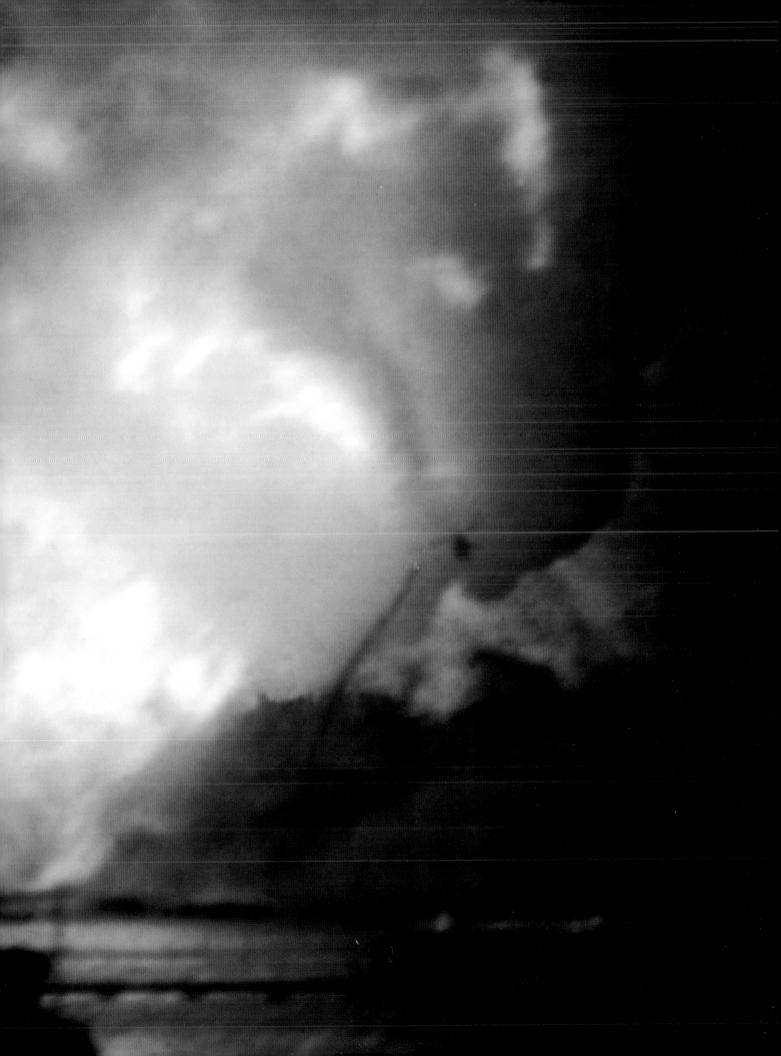

The *Akagi* ("Red Castle") was Admiral Nagumo's flagship. The Japanese used six carriers for their attack on Pearl Harbor. [USS *Arizona* Memorial]

A mock-up of Battleship Row at Ford Island was used by the Japanese for planning the attack on Pearl Harbor. [USS *Arizona* Memorial]

A Japanese Nakajima B5N high-level bomber carrying an 800-kg (1,760 lbs.) armor-piercing bomb.
[USAR 2420]

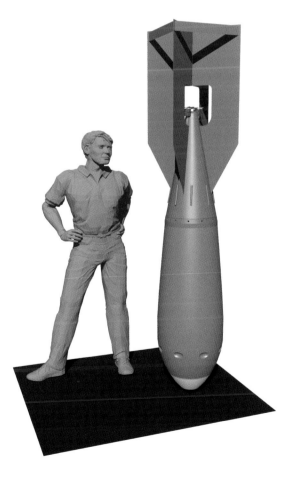

A Japanese Mitsubishi A6M "Zero" fighter takes off from the *Akagai*. About 350 aircraft would attack the U.S. military on Hawaii in two waves.
[U.S. National Archives, 80-G-182252]

The bomb that destroyed the *Arizona* was an 800-kg (1,760 lbs.) armor-piercing bomb dropped from a high-altitude bomber. Almost eight feet in length, the bomb carried only about 50 lbs of explosive, but that was enough to detonate the *Arizona's* forward ammunition magazines.
[Image by Andy Hall / Courtesy of the PAST Foundation]

The tipped foremast of the *Arizona* after she has settled on the harbor's bottom. [USS *Arizona* Memorial Photo Collection, USAR-12]

Watch Video:

Survivor Stories & Underwater World

Please see instructions on page 2.

At the time of the attack, the *Arizona* was moored at berth F-7, with the repair ship *Vestal* moored alongside. The vessel suffered hits from several bombs and was strafed. At about 8:05 a.m., the battleship took a death blow. A high-altitude bomber dropped a 1,760-lb bomb. The projectile hurtled through the air, reportedly striking near turret No. 2 and penetrating deep into the battleship's innards before exploding near the forward magazine. In a tremendous blast, the *Arizona* exploded. In an instant, most of the men aboard were killed, including Rear Admiral Isaac C. Kidd and Captain Franklin Van Valkenburgh, both posthumously awarded the Medal of Honor. The blast from the *Arizona* blew men off the decks of surrounding ships and threw tons of debris, including parts of bodies, all over the harbor. Survivors of the attack also claimed that the *Arizona* was hit by one or possibly two torpedoes. In any case, the battleship was utterly devastated from in front of her first turret back into her machinery spaces. Her sides were blown out and the turrets, conning tower,

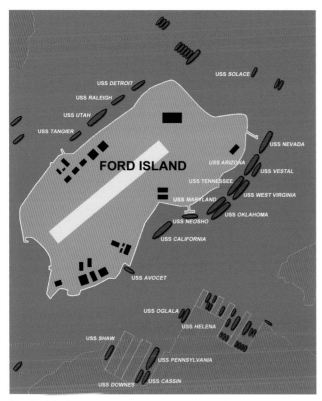

Battleship Row at 8:00 a.m. The *Arizona* is moored next to the repair ship *Vestal*.
[Illustration by author / Source: NPS]

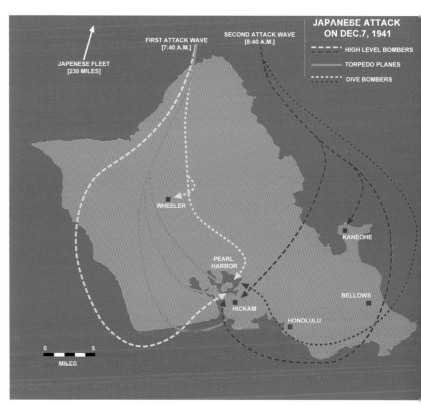

Route of the Japanese attack planes on December 7, 1941.
[Illustration by author / Source: NPS]

and much of the super-structure dropped several feet into her wrecked hull. This tipped her foremast forward, giving the wreck its distinctive appearance.

Abandoned at 10:32 a.m., the ship's burning super-structure and canted masts loomed through the smoke that blanketed the harbor. The wreck burned for al-most three days. Credit for the hit was officially given to Japanese pilot Tadashi Kusumi from the aircraft carrier *Hiryu*. The blast that destroyed the *Arizona* and sank her at her berth alongside of Ford Island consumed the lives of 1,177 men—over half of the casualties suffered by the entire fleet in the attack.

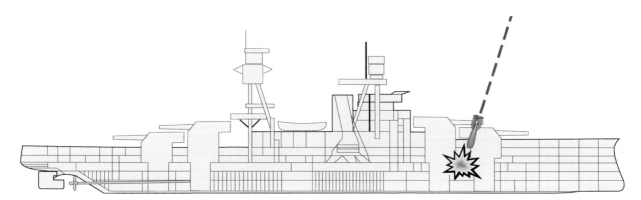

Illustration of the fatal bomb hit on the *Arizona's* forward magazines.
[Illustration by Author / Source: U.S. National Park Service]

Aerial view from a Japanese bomber from 10,000 feet over Battleship Row. The *Arizona* (second from left, inboard) is still afloat. Note the oil leaking from the damaged ships. This is probably the last photograph of the *Arizona* before her explosion.
[USAR-82]

In this view from a Japanese aircraft during the first wave of the attack, a plume from a torpedo explosion can be seen at center, alongside the battleships *Oklahoma* which ultimately capsized. A Japanese torpedo plane can be seen banking around just to the right of the plume. Moments after this photograph was taken, the *Arizona* was hit by the deadly 800-kg (1,760 lbs) bomb dropped by a high-level bomber.
[USAR-81]

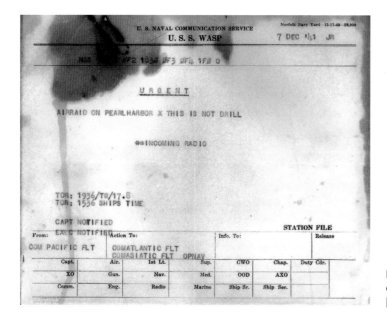

Naval dispatch informing about the attack on Pearl Harbor.
[U.S.Navy]

The death of the *Arizona* at approximately 8:05 a.m. on December 7, 1941. Frame clipped from a color motion picture taken by Captain Eric Haakensen from the hospital ship *Solace* (AH-5). [USAR-68]

FRONT BOW VIEW

BLACK POWDER MAGAZINES

UPPER DECK

MAIN DECK

SECOND DECK

THIRD DECK

FIRST PLATFORM

SECOND PLATFORM

HOLD

STARBOARD   PORTSIDE

14-INCH AMMUNITION MAGAZINES

The explosion reached the ship's forward oil bunkers and caused a massive fire at the ship's front turrets. This fire reached the powder magazines below through an open hatch and ignited the ship's black powder, thus sealing *Arizona's* fate.
[Illustration by author / Source: NPS]

Torpedo planes attack Battleship Row at about 8:00 a.m. on December 7, 1941, seen from a Japanese aircraft. Ships are, from lower left to right: the Nevada with flag raised at stern; *Arizona* with *Vestal* outboard; *Tennessee* with *West Virginia* outboard; *Maryland* with *Oklahoma* outboard; the fleet oiler *Neosho* and *California*. *West Virginia*, *Oklahoma*, and *California* have been torpedoed, as marked by ripples and spreading oil, and the first two are listing to port. Torpedo drop splashes and running tracks are visible at left and center.
[U.S. National Archives, 80-G-30550]

The *Arizona* after her explosion with the smoke covering the other ships. [USS *Arizona* Memorial]

USS *ARIZONA* SURVIVOR ACCOUNTS
John D. Anderson, Boatswain's Mate 2nd Class

Battleship Row in flames and smoke. Most of the battleships hit by bombs and torpedos settled on the shallow bottom of the harbor.
[U.S. Naval Historical Center, NH 97398]

John D. Anderson (above) and his twin brother Delbert who did not survive the attack on Pearl Harbor.
[Courtesy of John D. Anderson]

John D. Anderson was born on August 26, 1917, in Verona, South Dakota. He enlisted in the U.S. Navy in 1937. After basic training he was assigned to the aircraft carrier USS *Saratoga* and then to the USS *Arizona*. John Anderson volunteered for service in China in the First Squadron of destroyers with landing forces in Tsingtao, Chefo, and Swato. Since his twin brother Delbert was on the USS *Arizona*, he asked for and received transfer to that ship. Delbert Anderson did not survive the December 7, 1941 attack.

More than seven decades ago, a tragic event occurred that changed the course of history on this planet. The attack affected all of us who were alive at that time and to the present. In my case it was the loss of my twin brother—both of us were on the USS *Arizona*. He was a gun captain on an anti-aircraft battery on the starboard side of the boat deck, and was killed there. As sar as I know his remains were never found or identified. In the course of this battle I tried to get up on the boat deck to assist his gun crew but I never made it, and spent the next hours under fire rescuing other wounded and recovering the dead.

When the bombs began to drop on us, the crew went to their battle stations according to the watch station bill, and prepared to fire. Turret No. 4 was manned and ready when a bomb hit the face plate, bounced off, and penetrated the armored deck on its way to the interior of the ship, where it exploded in the C.I.C. with great loss of life. About this time Turret Captain Campbell called down to the gun pit for two men to drop down below into the magazine to see if the doors to this facility were jammed or still operable, and to report if water was coming in. Two sailors went below to check (one was Goodwin, the other person's name I do not remember).

Shortly thereafter, the unknown sailor reported what he found, but I did not see Goodwin. The power to the turret was knocked out and battle lanterns were not available; it was hard to see anyone. Dewayne Barth, John Evans, and Charlie Guerin were in the gun pit along with me and Clarence Otterman, Lewis Pacitti, and Jim Green. I then talked to Turret Captain Campbell about going out and aiding my twin brother's gun crew, as we knew the attack was being carried out by aircraft. He said "go for it," so I left the turret and headed for the boat deck. John Evans, Dewayne Barth, and Charles Guerin also dropped out the trap door to the main deck and got busy fighting fires and pulling burned and wounded people out of harm's way.

Guerin grasped an ax off the barbette and used it to chop the lines to the USS *Vestal*, which was moored next to the *Arizona*. When I reached the ladder to the boat deck, there was a massive blast of heat and fire, the metal was red hot, and the fire mains were knocked

out. Fire extinguishers were of little use at this time. An aircraft came in low, strafing the decks and causing more casualties. A small boat came alongside to starboard and we loaded dead and wounded men into the boat, the coxswain's name was Alexander. He took these men to the bunker on the northeastern corner of Ford Island, where they were loaded onto a flatbed truck and hauled away to a hospital or first aid station. Alexander came back alongside and we put in more wounded or dead that we could find on the burning ship.

Lt. Cdr. Fuqua was the senior officer there and finally called to abandon ship. He said for me to get in the boat, but I said no, my brother was still on board. Fuqua replied that my brother could not have

survived the explosions and heat, then he shoved me onto the boat along with a terribly burned sailor I was carrying. John Evans fell in and Guerin, Dewayne Barth, Clarence Otterman, and Lewis Pacitti were also on the boat when we took off for Ford Island. Goodwin was not in the boat with us, but John and I rescued Riefert on the way in. He was covered with oil and swimming in the fire, but we did save him (he later was assigned to a destroyer tender).

When I got ashore at the bunker, a number of troops were standing at the bunker's entrance looking out at the catastrophe. One of the sailors was Rose. Out in the harbor astern of the *Arizona* was a whaleboat adrift. I asked Rose, if he was game to swim out, get in, and head

back to the *Arizona*. He said he would, so we swam out, got the boat, started, and moved alongside the port quarter. Rose held the boat alongside while I went aboard. By this time the main deck was awash. I opened a hatch over the Admiral's galley and released a messman named Cruz, who, I later learned, survived the war. Then on to men burned beyond recognition, some body parts, and some whole persons, loaded them in our whale boat and took off for Hospital Point. On the way, as coxswain of the boat, we decided to stop at the USS *West Virginia*. From there we were told to carry out our orders, orders we did not have.

So I headed down the channel south, parallel to Ford Island, passing all battleships in various stages of

John D. Anderson (right) with his former shipmate Louis A. Conter during the Pearl Harbor Commemoration in 2014. Daniel Martinez in the background.
[U.S. Navy photo by Laurie Dexter]

damage. The second wave of enemy planes showed up as we came close to the seaplane ramp. Here we were hit, smashing our small craft, and we went into the water. After swimming around trying to get any survivors, I could find none. I did not find Rose, so I have to assume here is where he died.

I finally swam to shore and collapsed; after a short while, and with some urgency caused by strafing planes, I took off and found a rifle and two bandoliers of ammo leaning against a tree. This produced a certain feeling of security and then I started walking towards the bunker, going down the runway on Ford Island. I ran into a sailor from the *Arizona*, Walt Gaskins. Walt had on a complete dress uniform of the U.S. Marines and a .50-caliber machine gun. We found a hole in the runway and parked for the night. That night, carrier planes from the USS *Enterprise* came in to land and ran into a hail of fire. All the planes but one were knocked down. Everyone thought they were enemy's.

The next day a Marine patrol took our weapons and said that survivors should report to the 10-10 dock for muster. When Gaskins and I got there, all we saw was walking wounded or burned seamen. We were asked to volunteer for ships understaffed, so what was left of our navy could get out to sea.

Captain Gieselman would not let *Arizona* survivors all man one ship. All members were volunteers for any ship short of men. I volunteered and was sent to the destroyer *MacDonough* (DD-351). In all this time I did not see Goodwin. This was a tumultuous time, where everyone did their duty and became instant veterans from there on."

During the war John Anderson volunteered and participated in numerous campaigns, including the raids at Makin Salamaua, Lae, Truk, and Palau, the battle of the Solomon Islands, and Santa Cruz, the Aleutians, Tarawa, Saipan, the Philippines, Guam, Leyte Gulf, Iwo Jima, and Okinawa. After World War II he worked in motion picture studios in Hollywood, and graduated from the Martin School of Science. He later worked in the radio and TV broadcasting industry at KSWS TV, Roswell, New Mexico. In 1962 Mr. Anderson was invited to participate in the dedication ceremony for the USS *Arizona* Memorial. He married in 1968 and he and his wife Karolyn have three children. John Anderson retired from the Navy Reserve in 1976 and lives in Roswell, New Mexico.

Edward L. Wentzlaff, Aviation Ordnance Man 2nd Class

[Courtesy of Edward L. Wentzlaff]

Edward L. Wentzlaff was born on November 16, 1917 at Nicollet, Minnesota. After joining the U.S. Navy in 1937 he went to training at the Great Lakes and on to Electronics Ordnance School in San Diego, California. Edward Wentzlaff served aboard the *Arizona* in the V-3 division from 1938 until December 7, 1941.

"On the morning of Sunday, December 7, 1941 my best friend Walter Boviall and I congregated by turret No. 2, with about ten others waiting for the 8:00 a.m. church service. At this time we sighted the first Japanese plane, followed by more. The Japanese planes began curving into our battleship line and started strafing us. This was the first wave of attack and we were on the foc'sle [forecastle], which is the upper forward deck. The navigation, captain, admiral, are all located here. This is where the ship is controlled. Because we were being attacked, we were ordered below deck. I was at the end of the group of guys who went down the hatch, everybody went down except me, about eleven or twelve of the crew. I never saw any of them again, including my best friend Walter Boviall.

Instead of going below deck, I went to my battle station, at the quarterdeck; it was called repair one. I proceeded through the marine division, up to the quarterdeck where some of the men were sleeping. I went through their department and woke up a bunch of them; they had been on liberty from the previous day. I tried to warn them that we were being attacked. One guy said, "Oh it's nothing, it's the Army simulating." From time to time the Army would simulate a Sunday morn-

Boats search for survivors in the water.
[USS *Arizona* Memorial]

ing attack. Meanwhile, as Ford Island was on fire, four of us were scrambling for fire hoses (Lane, Hurst, Fuhr, and I) aboard the *Arizona*. The first raid lasted 45 minutes to an hour. We supposedly got eight torpedo and five bomb hits. Prior to the second wave of attack we were manning a fire hose by turret No. 3. The water main for the fire hose was being manned by Glenn Lane and I was unfolding and undoing the hose and holding the nozzle. We were getting no water pressure. I then traded places with Glenn Lane to work on the valves and

he was at the forward end of the hose when the ship exploded. Here is where the 1875-pound bomb went into the No. 2 magazine and the whole ship exploded, killing 1,177 on board. The whole area was covered with smoke and fire, you couldn't see a thing. At the point of the explosion, I had no idea what happened to either Glenn Lane or Milton Hurst. It was not until a subsequent anniversary that I saw them again.

As the second attack started, the crew of turret No. 3 started to climb out. They pulled me by the shirt and said, "...hey Wentzlaff,

let's get going." Between us and the *Arizona* was Ford Island. Everyone was abandoning ship. (Previous to the explosion, Admiral Kidd had returned to the *Arizona*. Admiral Kidd and Captain Van Valkenburgh were killed during the attack, along with most of the officers and the 1,177 crew.) We went to the enlisted men's gangway where we found ten to fifteen badly burned men. They had been burned black from the fire and smoke. The only thing left on them was the top of their shoes (the concussion was so strong it blew the soles off of their shoes) and

the band that holds their skivvies. All of their hair was burned off as well. To get the men off the ship I chopped off the line holding the admiral's barge from the ship. The *Arizona* was sinking and pulling the barge down with it. We took the seriously burned men from the gangway to the hospital ship USS *Solace* and returned to Ford Island. As we returned from the *Solace* we were ordered to take a motor launch around the ships and pick up the wounded and take them to the naval hospital.

Afterwards we came back to Ford Island and

Explosion of the forward magazines of the destroyer USS *Shaw*. The battleship *Nevada*, also hit by the attackers, is at right.
[USS *Arizona* Memorial]

they put us into work forces. The first one I went on was to the *West Virginia*, where they pumped water from one side to the other, so it wouldn't roll over. We were able to balance the ship and then sink it on an even keel. This ship was later repaired and went back into action in the Pacific.

After we got to the shipyard, they brought us to the recreation hall and issued us a rifle (30 calibers), ammunition, blanket, and food. It was now nearing the end of the first day. It was getting dark; we were sitting around the outside of the building. Earlier in the day we painted all of the windows black in this building. About an hour and a half later airplanes started coming into Ford Island. We were not aware of the origin of these planes. As they were coming in we all started shooting at these planes. We thought the Japanese were returning. We shot five planes down and killed three of the pilots. It was after we shot down five we realized they were off one of our carriers, the USS *Enterprise*. The pilots and the crew of the *Enterprise* did not know we had been attacked, and we did not know who they were. We unwittingly shot them down and killed them. We were expecting the Japanese to come back at anytime during the next three days. Once we had been attacked, our patrol boats and ship patrols circulated the area, patrolling a 1,500-mile radius."

After the attack on Pearl Harbor Edward Wentzlaff was assigned to the antisubmarine squadron and eventually to the aircraft carrier *Yorktown* which was later sunk at Midway. Later in the war he was stationed at Chimcotague Island, Virginia, training the air group for the carrier Roosevelt and was discharged in 1946 as a CWO-gunner. His World War II awards include the Navy and Marine Corps Medal. After the war Edward Wentzlaff married Alice J. Mork and raised 5 children. He served as the mayor of Butterfield, Minnesota and later as a Watonwan County Commissioner after retiring from farming. He presently lives in Milaca, Minnesota and is enjoying retirement. Edward Wentzlaff has made plans to be cremated and be buried aboard the *Arizona* with his former shipmates. He passed away in 2013.

Glenn H. Lane, Aviation Ordnance Man 2nd Class

[Courtesy of Glenn L. Lane]

Glenn H. Lane was born on January 29, 1918, in Williams, Iowa. He was active in boy scouts, baseball, basketball, and track. After graduation from high school in Plymouth, Iowa, in 1935 as second in his class, he spent two years in the C.C.C. (Civilian Conservation Corp) before joining the U.S. Navy in 1940. Glenn Lane was Honor Man of his company in boot camp and then attended Aviation Radio School in San Diego, California. Upon completion he was assigned to the Observation Squadron 1 aboard the *Arizona*. Here he served as an air crewman aboard the observation scout plane. Glenn Lane was aboard during the attack; was blown overboard by the explosions, and swam to the battleship *Nevada*, and was aboard her when she was sunk.

"When the attack started on December 7, 1941, just before 8:00 a.m., I was on the forecastle of the USS *Arizona*. I saw torpedo planes, with the Rising Sun insignia under their wings, attacking ships ahead of us. General alarm was sounded and we were all told to seek cover.

I went aft to the aviation workshop and helped wake men who were still sleeping there and I closed battle ports in the optical shop. The order came for all hands not assigned to anti-aircraft batteries to go to the third deck. I started for the third deck but just then general quarters was sounded. I came back and started for my general quarters station, a repair station (Patrol 5). We were hit aft and also in one or two other places on the ship.

Word came: "fire in the Executive Officer's office." Hurst, Bruns, Wentzlaff, and I manned a fire hose and went on the quarterdeck to connect it and fight the fire aft on the quarterdeck where the bomb had hit us. Lieutenant Commander Fuqua was at his post on the quarterdeck. I was on the nozzle end of the hose and told Hurst and Bruns to turn on the water. They did, but no water came. I turned around to see if the hose had any kinks in it and at that moment there was an explosion which knocked me off the ship.

I was picked up and taken aboard the *Nevada* where I was brought to my senses in a casemate (No. 3). I had been in the water because I was soaked with oil. The *Nevada* was underway and I helped handle powder for the 5-inch gun. When the *Nevada* was hit in the dry dock channel, the gun was put out and the ship was afire. I helped move the wounded aft and fought fire until I was choked by smoke and fumes. They sent me from the *Nevada* to the *Solace* where I was put to bed and had several cuts and bruises treated. I couldn't see, either, until my eyes were washed out and treated. I was released from the Solace December 10, and was sent to Receiving Barracks. There Mr. Fuqua told me to rejoin the aviation unit at Ford Island. I saw no signs of fear on the ship. Everyone was surprised, though, and pretty mad."

After the attack on Pearl Harbor, Glenn Lane served as air crewman on dive bombers, torpedo planes and scouting aircraft for the balance of the war. He continued to serve in the U.S. Navy for a total of thirty years, retiring in 1969 as Command Master Chief at Naval Air Station Whidbey. Glenn Lane and his wife, Beverly, raised six children and made their home in Oak Harbor, Washington. He passed away in 2011.

Radioman's Mate 3rd Class Glenn H. Lane hooks the OS2U Kingfisher seaplane on the ship's crane. The crane then lifted the plane back aboard the *Arizona*. This photo was taken on September 6, 1941, three months before the attack on Pearl Harbor.
[USAR-842]

Earl C. Nightingale, Corporal, U.S. Marine Corps

[NPS]

Earl Nightingale was born in Los Angeles, California, on March 12, 1921. At the age of seventeen he joined the United States Marines. He was on the *Arizona* during the attack on Pearl Harbor and was one of twelve surviving Marines aboard that day.

"At approximately 8:00 a.m. on the morning of December 7, 1941, I was leaving the breakfast table when the ship's siren for air defense sounded. Having no antiaircraft battle station, I paid little attention to it. Suddenly I heard an explosion. I ran to the port door leading to the quarterdeck and saw a bomb strike a barge of some sort alongside the *Nevada*, or in that vicinity. The Marine color guard came in at this point, saying we were being attacked. I could distinctly hear machine gun fire. I believe it was then that our antiaircraft battery opened up. We stood around awaiting orders of some kind.

General quarters sounded and I started for my battle station in secondary aft. As I passed through casement No. 9 I noted the gun was manned and being trained out. The men seemed extremely calm and collected. I reached the boat deck where our antiaircraft guns were in full action, firing very rapidly. I was about three quarters of the way to the first platform on the mast when it seemed as though a bomb struck our quarterdeck. I could hear shrapnel or fragments whistling past me. As soon as I reached the first platform, I saw Second Lieutenant Simonsen lying on his back with blood on his shirt front. I bent over him, and taking him by the shoulders, asked if there was anything I could do. He was dead, or so nearly so that speech was impossible. Seeing there was nothing I could do for him, I continued to my battle station. When I arrived in secondary aft I reported to Major Shapley that Mr. Simonsen had been hit and there was nothing to be done for him. There was a lot of talking going on and I shouted for silence, which came immediately. I had only been there a short time when a terrible explosion caused the ship to shake violently. I looked at the boat deck and everything seemed aflame forward of the mainmast. I reported to Major Shapley that the ship was aflame, which was rather needless, and after looking about, he ordered us to leave. I was the last man to leave secondary aft because I looked around to check and there was no one left.

I followed Major Shapley down the port side of the tripod mast. The railings, as we ascended, were very hot and as we reached the boat deck I noted that it was torn up and burned. The bodies of the dead were thick, and badly burned men were heading for the quarterdeck, only to fall apparently dead or badly wounded. Major Shapley and I went between No. 3 and No. 4 turret to the starboard side and found Lt. Cmdr. Fuqua ordering the men over the side and assisting the wounded. He seemed exceptionally calm and Major Shapley stopped and they talked for a moment. Charred bodies were everywhere. I made my way to the quay and started to remove my shoes when I suddenly found myself in the water. I think the concussion of a bomb threw me in. I started swimming for the pipeline, about one hundred and fifty feet away. I was about halfway there when my strength gave out entirely. My clothes and shocked condition sapped my strength, and I was about to go under when Major Shapley started to swim by, and seeing my distress, grasped my shirt and told me to hang on to his shoulders while he swam in. We were perhaps twenty-five feet from the pipeline when his strength gave out and I saw he was floundering, so I loosened my grip on him and told him to make it alone. He stopped and grabbed me by the shirt and refused to let go. I would have drowned but for Major Shapley. We finally reached the beach where a Marine directed us to a bomb shelter, where I was given dry clothes and a place to rest."

Before being mustered out of the Marine Corps after World War II, Earl Nightingale returned to the United States and became an instructor at Camp Lejeune, North Carolina. There he noticed a new radio station under construction, and applied for a job. He was hired by WJNC, and began his career as a motivational speaker and author. He was the voice in the early 1950s of *Sky King*, the hero of a radio adventure series, and was a WGN radio show host from 1950 to 1956. Earl Nightingale was the author of the *Strangest Secret*, one of the most successful motivational books of all time. After his retirement and before his death in March 1989, Earl Nightingale and his wife, Diana formed Keys Publishing.

Samuel G. Fuqua, Lieutenant Commander

[NPS]

Samuel Glenn Fuqua was born in Laddonia, Missouri, on 15 October 1899. After a year at the University of Missouri and World War I service in the Army, he entered the U.S. Naval Academy in July 1919. Following graduation and commissioning in June 1923, he served on the battleship *Arizona*, destroyer *McDonough* and battleship *Mississippi* before receiving shore duty at San Francisco, California, in 1930-32. Lieutenant Fuqua served on other ships and at shore stations during the mid-1930s, and was Commanding Officer of the minesweeper *Bittern* in the Asiatic Fleet in 1937-39. After service at the Naval Training Station, Great Lakes, Illinois, in 1939-41, Lieutenant Commander Fuqua returned to the *Arizona* as the ship's damage control officer and First Lieutenant, and was on board her on December 7, 1941. Though knocked unconscious by a bomb that hit the ship's stern early in the attack, he subsequently directed fire fighting and rescue efforts. After the ship's forward magazines exploded, he was her senior surviving officer and was responsible for saving her remaining crewmen. For his distinguished conduct and heroism at that

Stern view of the sunken *Arizona*. The smoke could be seen from miles away. In the background, men on the stern of the battleship *Tennessee* are playing fire hoses on the water to force the burning oil away from their ship.
[USS *Arizona* Memorial]

time, he was awarded the Medal of Honor.

"I was in the ward room eating breakfast at about 7:55 a.m., when a short signal on the ship's air raid alarm was made. I immediately went to the phone and called the officer-of-the-deck to sound general quarters and then shortly thereafter ran up to the starboard side of the quarterdeck to see if he had received word. On coming out of the ward room hatch on the portside, I saw a Japanese plane go by, the machine guns firing, at an altitude of about 100 feet. As I was running forward on the starboard side of the quarterdeck, approximately by the starboard gangway, I was apparently knocked out by the blast of a bomb which I learned later had struck the face plate of No. 4 turret on the starboard side and had glanced off and gone through the deck just forward of the captain's hatch, penetrating the decks and exploding on the third deck. When I came to and got up off the deck, the ship was a mass of flames amidships on the boat deck and the deck aft was awash to about frame 90. The antiaircraft battery and machine guns apparently were still firing at this time. Some of the *Arizona's* boats had pulled clear of the oil and were lying off the stern. At this time I attempted, with the assistance of the crews of No. 2 and No. 4 turrets, to put out the fire which was coming from the boat deck

and which had extended to the quarterdeck. There was no water on the fire mains. However, about fourteen CO2s were obtained that were stowed on the port side and held the flames back from the quarterdeck, enabling us to pick up wounded who were running down the boat deck out of the flames. I placed about seventy wounded and injured in the boats that had been picked up off the deck aft and landed them at Ford Island. This task was completed by about 9:00 or 9:30 a.m.

Not knowing whether the captain or the admiral had ever reached the bridge, I had the Captain's hatch opened up, immediately after I came to, and sent Ensign G. B. Lennig, U.S.N.R. and Ensign J. D. Miller, U.S.N. down to search the Captain's and Admiral's cabins to see if they were there. By this time, both those cabins were about waist deep in water. A search of the two cabins revealed that the admiral and captain were not there. Knowing that they were on board I assumed that they had proceeded to the bridge. All personnel but three or four men, from turrets No. 3 and No. 4, were saved. At about 9:00 a.m., seeing that all guns of the antiaircraft and secondary battery were out of action and that the ship could not possibly be saved, I ordered all hands to abandon ship. From information received from other personnel on board, I learned that

a bomb had struck the forecastle, just about the time the air raid siren sounded at 7:55 a.m. A short interval thereafter, there was a terrific explosion on the forecastle, apparently from the bomb penetrating the magazine. Approximately thirty seconds later a bomb hit the boat deck, just forward of the stack. One went down the stack, and one hit the faceplate of No. 4 turret indirectly.

The commanding officer of the *Vestal* stated that two torpedoes passed under his vessel, which was secured alongside the *Arizona*, and struck the ship. The first attack occurred about 7:55 a.m. I saw approximately fifteen torpedo planes come in to the attack from the direction of the Navy Yard. These planes also strafed the ship after releasing their torpedoes. Shortly thereafter there followed a dive bomber and strafing attack by about thirty planes. This attack was very determined, planes diving within 500 feet before releasing bombs, at about 9:00 a.m. There were about twelve planes in flight that I could see. The personnel of the antiaircraft and machine gun batteries on the *Arizona* lived up to the best traditions of the Navy. I could hear guns firing on the ship long after the boat deck was a mass of flames. I cannot single out one individual who stood out in acts of heroism above the others; all of the personnel under my supervision conducted themselves with the

greatest heroism and bravery."

During most of 1942, Samuel Fuqua was an officer of the cruiser *Tuscaloosa.* In 1943 and 1944, he was assigned to duty at Guantanamo Bay, Cuba, and attended the Naval War College. Captain Fuqua was operations officer for the commander of the Seventh Fleet from January to August 1945, helping to plan and execute several amphibious operations in the Philippines and Borneo area. After World War II he served in other staff positions. From 1949 to 1950 he commanded the destroyer tender *Dixie.* After service as the Chief of Staff of the Eighth Naval District, he retired from active duty in July 1953, receiving at that time the rank of Rear Admiral on the basis of his combat awards. Rear Admiral Samuel G. Fuqua passed away at Decatur, Georgia, on January 27, 1987.

Donald A. Graham, Aviation Machinist's Mate 1st Class

Donald Alexander Graham was born in Scranton, Lackawanna County, Pennsylvania, on June 17, 1900.

When the Japanese attacked Pearl Harbor he was a aviation machinist's mate on board the *Arizona*: "On hearing the explosions and gun reports, E. Wentzlaff, AOM2c, came in saying we were being attacked and bombed by Japanese planes. The air raid siren sounded, followed by the alarm. I stepped outside the shop and started to my general quarters station on the quarterdeck shouting, "Let's go." It seemed as though the magazines forward blew up while we were hooking up the fire hose, as the noise was followed by an awful "swish" and hot air blew out of the compartments. There had been bomb hits at the first start and yellowish smoke was pouring out of the hatches from below deck. There were lots of men coming out on the quarterdeck with every stitch of clothing and shoes blown off, painfully burned and shocked. Lt. Cmdr. Fuqua was the senior officer on deck and set an example for the men by being unperturbed, calm, cool, and collected, exemplifying the courage and traditions of an officer under fire. It seemed like the men, though painfully burned, shocked, and dazed, became inspired and took things in stride, seeing Lt. Cmdr. Fuqua seeming so unconcerned about the bombing and strafing, standing on the quarterdeck. There was no one going to pieces or growing panicky noticeable, as Lt. Cmdr. Fuqua directed the moving of the wounded and burned men from the quarterdeck to the motor launches and boats. He gave orders to get the life rafts on No. 3 barbette down, supervised the loading of the wounded and burned casualties, assisted by Ensign J. D. Miller, who set a very good example for a younger officer by being cool, calm, and collected. The signal gang, quartermasters, and all hands on the bridge went up as the signal men were trying to put out a fire in the signal rack and grabbing signal flags out to hoist a signal, the whole bridge went up, flames enveloping and obscuring them from view, the flames shooting upward twice as high as the tops.

A bomb hit on the starboard side of the after 5-inch guns and antiaircraft gun, and got most of the Marine crew and antiaircraft crews. It seemed

The *Arizona's* collapsed foremast afire as seen from Ford Island. At left are the ship's mainmast and boat cranes which remained widely intact after the explosion.
[Hawaii State Archives]

The *Arizona* in the late afternoon with her stern section largely intact and the National Ensign still flying. It was lowered later that day.
[USAR-63]

as though one bomb hit the port after the antiaircraft crew and came down through the casemate and executive officer's office. After the big explosion and "swish," the men painfully burned and wounded, dazed beyond comprehension, came out on the quarterdeck. I had to stop some of them from entering the flames later on and directed them over to the starboard side of the deck to the gangway for embarking, encouraging them to be calm. The *Vestal*, tied up alongside the portside, did not seem to get hit hard and started to get underway. I stood by to cast off lines on the quarterdeck portside and cast off their bow lines, as Lt. Cmdr. Fuqua on her wanted to save the line to tie up to one of the buoys.

Assisted by a seaman from No. 4 turret, I rendered the bow line around and cast her off. Then, getting the small life raft on No. 3 turret barbette portside off and over the port stern, the water and oil being on deck, and the ship settling fast, we got orders to embark in the motor boat at the starboard stern quarter, Lt. Cmdr. Fuqua and a few others still being aboard. We landed at B.O.Q. landing, Ford Island. Smith, a boat coxswain, made many trips for wounded and burned men being delivered by Lt. Cmdr. Fuqua, still on board. Courage and performance of all hands was of the highest order imaginable, especially considering the handicaps of adverse conditions and witnessing shipmates be-

ing blown up alongside them. There was no disorder, nor tendency to run around in confusion. The coolness and calm manner of Lt. Cmdr. Fuqua and Ensign J. D. Miller instilled confidence in the surviving crew."

On December 7, 1998, 57 years after the attack on Pearl Harbor, Rear Admiral William G. Sutton, Commander, Naval Base Pearl Harbor recalled a few of the men who survived the attack, whose actions exemplified the Navy's core values of honor, courage and commitment. "Aboard the *Arizona*, Aviation Machinist's Mate 1st Class Donald Graham braved intense flames and machine gun fire, to release the lines connecting the battleship with the repair ship USS

Vestal. Graham's actions allow the Vestal to get underway to safety."

Donald Graham was awarded the Navy Cross for his action on December 7, 1941.

He passed away in San Diego County, California, on February 11, 1976.

Captain Franklin Van Valkenburgh

Captain Franklin Van Valkenburgh was the *Arizona's* last commanding officer. He died on December 7, 1941 and was posthumously awarded the Medal of Honor. In 1943, the destroyer USS *Van Valkenburgh* (DD-656) was named in his honor.
[U.S. Naval Historical Center]

Franklin Van Valkenburgh was born in Minneapolis, Minnesota on April 5, 1888. Appointed a midshipman in 1905, he graduated from the U.S. Naval Academy four years later. His initial service was aboard battleships, punctuated by a tour with the Asiatic Squadron from 1911 to 1914. Van Valkenburgh received his postgraduate education in the field of steam engineering and became engineering officer of the battleship *Rhode Island* during World War I. He was twice an instructor at the Naval Academy during the late 1900s through the 1920s and served on the battleships *Minnesota* and *Maryland* during that time. Following promotion to the rank of commander, he was assigned to the office of the chief of naval operations in Washington, D.C. from 1928 to 1931. In the early 1930s, Commander Van Valkenburgh was in charge of the destroyer *Talbot* and Destroyer Squadron 5. He was a student at the U.S. Naval War College and inspector of naval material at the New York Navy Yard before he became the commanding officer of the destroyer tender *Melville* from 1936 to 1938. Captain Van Valkenburgh then spent a tour ashore with the 3rd Naval District and in February 1941 became commanding officer of the *Arizona*. He was killed in action when his ship exploded and sank during the attack on Pearl Harbor on December 7, 1941. For his "conspicuous devotion to duty and extraordinary courage" at that time, he was posthumously awarded the Medal of Honor. The destroyer *Van Valkenburgh* (DD-656) was named in his honor.

Rear Admiral Isaac C. Kidd

Rear Admiral Kidd died on his flagship *Arizona*.
[U.S. Naval Historical Center]

Isaac Kidd was born in Cleveland, Ohio on March 26, 1884. He entered the U.S. Naval Academy in 1902, graduating with the class of 1906. Kidd participated in the "Great White Fleet" cruise around the world from 1907 to 1909 while serving on the battleship *New Jersey*. Following service on the battleship *North Dakota* and the cruiser *Pittsburgh*, he was aide and flag secretary to the commander-in-chief of the Pacific Fleet, the first of his many flagstaff assignments. He also was an instructor at the Naval Academy between 1916 and 1917. During and after World War I, Kidd was stationed on the battleship *New Mexico*, and had further staff and Naval Academy service. He became executive officer of the battleship *Utah* from 1925 to 1926, and then commanded the replenishment ship *Vega*. He then became captain of the port at Cristóbal, Panama Canal Zone. Promoted to the rank of captain, Kidd worked as chief of staff to Commander, Base Force, and U.S. Fleet from 1930 to 1932. After three years at the Bureau of Navigation in Washington, D.C., he was commander of Destroyer Squadron 1, Scouting Force, from 1935 to 1936. Captain Kidd then attended the U.S. Naval War College and served on the college's staff before he became the commanding officer of the *Arizona* in 1938. Two years later,

85

he was promoted to rear admiral and assigned as the commander of Battleship Division 1 and chief of staff to the commander of the Battleship Force. On December 7, 1941, he was killed in action on board the *Arizona*, his flagship. Rear Admiral Isaac C. Kidd was posthumously awarded the Medal of Honor for his actions during the attack on Pearl Harbor. Three ships were named in his honor.

The first USS *Kidd* (DD-661) was a *Fletcher*-class destroyer in World War II. Today the ship is a floating museum in Baton Rouge, Louisiana.
[U.S. Naval Historical Center]

President Franklin D. Roosevelt signs the declaration of war on Japan the day following the attack.
[USS *Arizona* Memorial]

Newspaper reporting the attack on Pearl Harbor.
[USS *Arizona* Memorial]

THE WHITE HOUSE
WASHINGTON

The President of the United States in the name of The Congress takes pride in presenting the MEDAL OF HONOR posthumously to

REAR ADMIRAL ISAAC C. KIDD
UNITED STATES NAVY

for service as set forth in the following

CITATION:

"For conspicuous devotion to duty, extraordinary courage, and complete disregard of his own life, during the attack on the Fleet in Pearl Harbor, Territory of Hawaii, by Japanese forces on December 7, 1941. He immediately went to the bridge and as Commander Battleship Division One courageously discharged his duties as Senior Officer Present Afloat until the U.S.S. ARIZONA, his Flagship, blew up from magazine explosions and a direct bomb hit on the bridge which resulted in the loss of his life."

/s/ Franklin D. Roosevelt

Citation awarded posthumously to Rear Admiral Isaac C. Kidd.
[U.S. Naval Historical Center, NH 42852-KN]

The Aftermath - Removal of Bodies

One question still haunts visitors to the USS *Arizona* Memorial to this day. Why were the dead not removed? Initially, about 105 bodies were removed but because the ship was never raised, the remainder could not. The priority at that time was salvage of ships that could be repaired, and the *Arizona* was not in that category. As a result, the bodies deteriorated to the point of not being identifiable. Even as late as 1947, requests were made in regard to removal of the dead, but were rejected. They are considered buried at sea by the U.S. Navy.

Aerial view of Battleship Row on December 10, 1941, showing the damage from the Japanese raid three days earlier. In the upper left corner is the sunken *California*, with smaller vessels clustered around her. Diagonally, from left center to lower right are: the *Maryland*, lightly damaged, with the capsized *Oklahoma* outboard (a barge is alongside the *Oklahoma*, supporting rescue efforts); the *Tennessee*, lightly damaged, with the sunken *West Virginia* outboard; the *Arizona*, lower right, is sunk, with her hull shattered by the explosion of the magazines below the two forward turrets. Note dark oil streaks on the harbor surface, originating from the sunken battleships.
[USAR-2273]

Pearl Harbor Survivor
Sterling R. Cale, Pharmacist's Mate 2nd Class

Sterling Cale as a pharmacist's mate at the Pearl Harbor Hospital in August 1941.
[Courtesy of Sterling R. Cale]

Sterling R. Cale was born in Macomb, Illinois on November 29, 1921. He enlisted for Lighter-Than-Air Training (Dirigibles) at Lakehurst, New Jersey. When the German airship, the Hindenburg, exploded and burned in 1937, the Navy Department cancelled its dirigible program. As a result, Sterling graduated instead as a hospital pharmacist's mate 2nd class from the naval school in San Diego, California. Sterling Cale was assigned to the U.S. Naval Hospital at "C" Landing, located at Pearl Harbor, where he was transferred to the shipyard dispensary in July of 1941. On the morning of December 7, 1941, he completed night duty. He arrived at the receiving station around

7:00 a.m., signed out with the master-at-arms, and went outside. Less than an hour later, he noticed planes diving on Battleship Row. Initially Sterling Cale believed it was another mock attack, until suddenly a plane turned off to the right, granting him a glimpse of the "Rising Sun" on the wing tips and fuselage. He gasped as he said,

This clock was located on the *Arizona's* quarter deck. It stopped at 10:05 a.m. on December 7, 1941. It was later recovered by Sterling Cale.
[Photo by author]

"My God, those are Japanese planes! We're being attacked!" Six days after the attack on Pearl Harbor, Sterling Cale was placed in charge of the burial detail responsible for removing

the bodies off of the *Arizona*.

"We had to take one of the surviving barges in the harbor to get over to the *Arizona*, which had burned for two and a half days. We found many men in little piles of ashes around the 5-inch/51-caliber guns and the 5-inch/25-caliber guns. There were remains of a Marine in the forward tower.

It was either the officer-of-the-day or in charge of the guns. The forward hatch was closed, a body below, helmets thrown forward in equal line, we did not find the head for the body. The

ashes were blowing across the deck and off the ship—we were unable to stop this or to retain any. This was my first big job on a battleship and I was unable to do anything about it. I sank back on my haunches in great consternation and surprise, and found myself in tears. A few minutes later, I realized that I had a job to do, my ten-man detail standing around waiting for my orders to carry on as a petty officer in charge of a burial detail. We found a number of men in the after mast who had entered the fire control ladder to escape by climbing up the ladder, but fire had caught them and they had been reduced to solid charcoal—about three feet each person and bunched together in one solid mass. They were so difficult to dissect that in attempting to spur them apart, a head or arm or a leg would come off a body before we could place them in a sea bag for a temporary burial at Red Hill. We spent some six weeks removing bodies, many of which were only piles of ashes. It was strange—no one was wearing any dog tags—although I know that each person was issued two tags at the training station, but because the tags were made of aluminum they must have been reduced to an unrecognizable object by the heat of the fire."

Sterling Cale spent World War II with the 1st Marine Division at Guadalcanal. He transferred to the U.S. Army in 1948. From 1950 to 1951, he carried out his assignment with the 5th Regimental Combat Team in Korea. From 1955 to 1974, Mr. Cale served in Vietnam, first as an army sergeant major and later as a civilian State Department employee. During this time, he also carried out intermediate assignments to the Defense Language Institute in Monterey, California. Sterling Cale graduated with an MBA from Chaminade University in Honolulu, in 1975. In March 2005, he retired with 57 years of government service. He started volunteering at the USS *Arizona* Memorial shortly after his retirement. Mr. Cale has been an active participant in the Pearl Harbor Survivor Series part of the Witness to History videoconferencing program. This series enables students on both a national and international level to learn about the December 7 attack by directly communicating with survivors.

Sterling Cale speaks at the 50th anniversary commemoration of the dedication of the USS *Arizona* Memorial, 2012. [Michael R. Holzworth, U.S. Department of Defense]

Arizona's cranes remained largely intact. Note the 5-inch guns in the foreground. [USS *Arizona* Memorial]

Sterling Cale and his men took this barge to get over to the sunken *Arizona* six days after the attack to recover human remains. [Courtesy of Sterling R. Cale]

Portside view of *Arizona's* burned-out superstructure which remained above the waterline. Sterling Cale and his men had to climb through the whole superstructure to recover the crew's remains.
[USAR-774]

With the collapsed foremast becoming a symbol of the attack on Pearl Harbor...

... it became part of various recruiting posters.
[USS *Arizona* Memorial]

SALVAGING THE *ARIZONA*

Close-up of the collapsed foremast area. The bridge has partly melted and settled onto the top of the armored conning tower. [USAR-405]

A derrick lifts away the foretop, May 1942. The ship's cranes are still on board.
[USAR-758]

The attack on Pearl Harbor left the Pacific Fleet in a state of chaos and impotence. Japan's goal had been achieved—the U.S. Navy was unable to oppose the Japanese invasion of Southwest Asia, the Philippines, and islands of the South Pacific. Twenty-one ships of the Pacific Fleet had been sunk or damaged. Of that number, eight battleships were casualties, five sunk and three damaged. The main battle line of the fleet was out of action. Of growing concern was the location and intention of the Japanese navy. Fleet commanders at Pearl Harbor ordered their officers to assemble a priority list of ships that could be put back into service. This would then allow the fleet the opportunity

The foretop after the removal of the battery control station. [USAR-755]

One of the cranes with the armored conning tower in the background. [USAR-781]

View from the mainmast showing the remains of the foremast. Note the bow the background.
[USAR-404]

The two aft gun turrets (No. 3 and No. 4) after the removal of the barrels except one, spring 1942.
[U.S. National Archives, 296940]

Removal of a 14-inch gun barrel.
[USAR-767]

to prepare for battle and form strategies. Of all the ships lost or damaged at Pearl Harbor, the *Arizona* offered the most pathetic sight. Despite the crumpled superstructure and main decks awash, divers began exploring the wreckage of the ship within a week. It was soon discovered that the after part of the ship, from the break in the deck to the stern, was relatively intact. Removal of safes, valuables, and documents of a sensitive nature had begun by early 1942. As-

sessment dives continued to evaluate the feasibility of raising the *Arizona*. Salvage officers initially considered building a cofferdam around the vessel's perimeter, thus sealing the ship off from the harbor to allow the pumping of water from interior spaces. Examination of the harbor's coral bottom concluded that it was too porous and would not allow this process. Throughout 1942 and 1943, examination dives continued inside and outside the ship. Meanwhile,

ordnance divers had begun to remove ammunition and projectiles in May 1942. Eventually guns, machinery, and other equipment were removed for use on other ships or stations. On May 5, 1942, the toppled foremast of the *Arizona* was cut away and removed. The mainmast was taken away by August 23. Other features removed were the stern aircraft crane (December 23) and the conning tower (December 30).

The U.S. Navy decided that the U.S. Army would

receive gun turrets No. 3 and 4 for use as coastal defense guns. Two sites were selected: one at Mokapu Head, known as Battery *Pennsylvania*, and the second at an area known today as Electric Hill (Hawaiian Electric Industries, HEI, generating plant) on the western shore of Oahu. Only Battery *Pennsylvania* was completed. A test firing took place four days before the surrender of Japan. Today both sites are abandoned; the guns were removed and cut up for

Salvage and removal of the rotating portion of gun turret No. 3, April 1943.
[USAR-406]

other work." In his mind, as well as others', the conviction had formed that the *Arizona* would never fight again. On December 1, 1942, the vessel was struck from the books of commissioned ships. By October 1943, the last salvage work was completed. The ship had been stripped down to the main deck; none of the graceful superstructure remained.

In 1961, the *Arizona* was altered once more. In order to place the present memorial over the ship, a section of the boat deck that rested over the galley amidships was cut away. Initially this had been the area of a flag and platform for ceremonies and visits to the site from 1950 to 1960. This portion of the *Arizona* was removed to Waipio Point where it remains today.

scrap shortly after the war ended. Despite the work done to remove all useful materials from the *Arizona*, it was apparent the ship itself was lost. A memorandum from the commandant of the Navy Yard to Washington in June 1942, suggested abandoning salvage work on the *Arizona* because it was a "task of great magnitude entailing the diversion of large numbers of men and equipment from

Removal of the gun slide from one of the two aft 14-inch gun turrets.
[USAR-778]

One of the salvaged analog computers which were used for target plotting.
[USAR-790]

The foundation of gun turret No. 3 is lifted clear of its barbette, April 1943.
[USAR-407]

The interior of the barbette of gun turret No. 3 after the removal of the foundation.
[USAR-410]

Close-up of the inside of gun turret No. 3 barbette after the removal of the upper section of the rotating section, April 1943.
[USAR-409]

Removal of the upper section of the rotating portion of one of the 14-inch gun turrets, May 1943.
[USAR-757]

The photograph illustrates the dangerous working conditions for the salvage workers inside the *Arizona*.
[USAR-1731]

Divers in front of the decompression chamber after emerging from the sunken ship.
[USAR-1732]

One of the salvaged 5-inch guns of the secondary armament.
[USAR-753]

Aerial view of the *Arizona* after the removal of her armament and superstructure, 1943.
[USAR-786]

A diver emerges from the interior of the *Arizona*.
[USAR-1731]

Members of the U.S. Navy visit the site of the *Arizona*'s relics. After their removal from the ship they found their final resting place near Pearl Harbor's West Loch.
(Joe Kane, U.S. Navy)

Arizona and Pearl Harbor survivors gather behind the exhibit featuring pieces of the *Arizona* at Camp John Paul Jones Recruit Training Command (RTC), Great Lakes, 2004.
[Michael A. Worner, U.S. Navy]

BUILDING THE MEMORIAL

The memorial was designed to give the appearance of floating gracefully over the *Arizona*. In truth, two 250-ton steel girders and 36 concrete pilings, driven deep into the bed of the harbor, support the building.
[Jacob Kohrs , U.S. Army]

Memorial service of the Pearl Harbor Navy Yard on the hulk of the sunken *Arizona* after the removal of her superstructure.
[Courtesy of Burl Burlingame]

The USS *Arizona* Memorial is the final resting place for the majority of her 1,177 sailors and Marines who lost their lives on December 7, 1941. The structure spanning the mid-portion of the sunken battleship was built to honor not only the fallen crew of the *Arizona*, but also for the members of the U.S. Armed Forces who died as a result of the attack on Pearl Harbor. The USS *Arizona* Memorial is one of America's most revered and sacred sites. It's a place of quiet contemplation, where visitors can reflect on the great sacrifice made by those who gave their lives to defend America's freedom. From the soaring beauty of the memorial to the aching reality of the men entombed in the ship that lies beneath, visitors from around the world experience a pervasive sense of loss with an enormous feeling of gratitude and pride.

O. R. Greer, National President of American War Dads, places a wreath on the *Arizona's* hulk honoring the perished battleship's crew members, 1948.
[Courtesy of Burl Burlingame]

Temporary Memorial 1950

The first formal recognition of the *Arizona* after the attack was on March 7, 1950, when Admiral Arthur Radford ordered that the American flag fly over the sunken battleship. Later that year a wooden platform was constructed over the midship area. Admiral Radford also ordered the raising and lowering of the American flag on a daily basis.

The first memorial for the *Arizona* erected in 1950.
[USAR-1702]

Aerial view of the first memorial built over the *Arizona*, early 1950s. She rests next to her mooring quays.
[USAR-512]

Fundraising

President Eisenhower signed Public Law 85-344 authorizing the creation of the USS *Arizona* Memorial on March 15, 1958. The Public Law stipulated that the monument would be built without federal funding. The Pacific War Memorial Commission (PWMC) was tasked with raising the $ 532,000 required to build the structure. The PWMC wrestled with concerns over the message and the appropriations of the proposed memorial for years before settling on the final design. Several organizations and individuals helped in the effort to raise the amount. In 1958, the Territory of Hawaii contributed the initial $50,000. On December 3, 1958, the popular television series "This is Your Life," hosted by Mr. Ralph Edwards, featured Medal of Honor Recipient Samuel Fuqua, the senior surviving officer from the *Arizona*. This broadcast kicked off the public fundraising campaign. Over $95,000 was raised for the new permanent structure. Three years later, on March 15, 1961, singing legend Elvis Presley hosted a benefit concert at Pearl Harbor's Block Arena, raising over $64,000. The Fleet Reserve Association (FRA) partnered with Revell Model Company to sell plastic models of the *Arizona*. The kit included a donation information printed on the instruction sheet. This led to the raising of $40,000. Finally, on September 6, 1961, freshman Hawaii Senator Daniel K. Inouye secured federal funding which contributed the final $150,000 to complete the construction. In the end, public money was required to meet the goal of the PWMC. The legislation stated that the memorial was "to be maintained in honor and commemoration of the members of the Armed Forces of the United States who gave their lives for their country during the attack on Pearl Harbor, Hawaii on December 7, 1941."

Elvis Presley on stage at his benefit performance at Pearl Harbor's Block Arena, March 25, 1961. The concert raised over $ 64,000 for the construction of the USS *Arizona* Memorial. [USAR-1678]

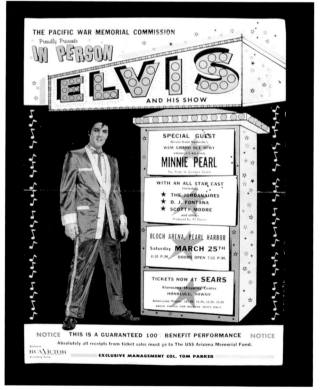

A poster announcing the benefit concert. [USS *Arizona* Memorial]

Concept

Renowned architect Alfred Preis designed the structure over the sunken ship. The gleaming, white memorial straddles, but does not touch the *Arizona*. The concave silhouette symbolizes America's initial defeat and ultimate victory in World War II. One feature purposely designed into the structure is the "Tree of Life", a universal symbol of renewal that also graces the entryway of the visitor center.

Architectual concept by G. Leonhart. This idea was rejected by the U.S. Navy. [USAR-166]

Alfred Preis's second conception for the memorial, 1959. His first idea, which would have allowed visitors to descend to a subsurface enclosure and view the wreck through an underwater window, was not accepted by the U.S. Navy. [USAR-165]

The schematics of Alfred Preis's accepted design. [USS *Arizona* Memorial]

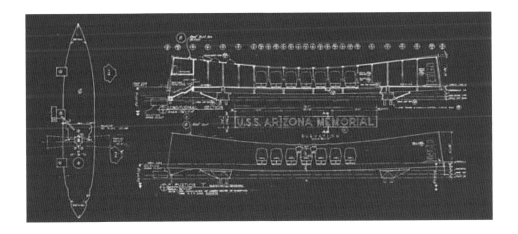

The Architect

Alfred Preis, photographed during the early 1960s.
[USS *Arizona* Memorial]

Alfred Preis's journey to Pearl Harbor began in 1939 shortly after Hitler had annexed his home country Austria. Born in 1911, he fled to the United States to escape the occupation of his native land. Eventually, he became established in Honolulu, Hawaii. After the attack on Pearl Harbor, Alfred Preis was arrested and detained as an enemy alien because his native country, Austria, was now part of the Axis powers. He was interned for several months at the Sand Island detainment camp. Eventually, Preis was released and he went to work for the U.S. Navy designing buildings to support the war effort. After the war was over, he established his own architectural firm in Honolulu. When the call for a design for a memorial was announced, Preis's firm competed for the opportunity. The Preis design for the memorial was selected in 1959. In that year, the first design he submitted was rejected. His second concept was accepted and construction began in 1960.

Alfred Preis speaks during the commemoration ceremony of the 50th anniversary of the Japanese attack on Pearl Harbor, December 1991.
[Gloria Montgomery, U.S. Navy]

Wooden frames were used to give the memorial its form.
[Hawaii State Archives]

Close-up of the roof construction.
[Hawaii State Archives]

The memorial in the early
stages of construction.
The base already has been
completed.
[USAR-1712]

The memorial nearing
completion, 1962. Note the
temporary flagstaff in the
foreground.
[Hawaii State Archives]

Preis viewed his architectural design as a bridge-like structure spanning, but not touching, the sunken battleship below. His design represents a serene atmosphere for contemplation. The memorial is divided into three distinct sections. The first section is the entry area that opened up into a small museum space, lit by three circular skylights. Passing through this section, one would come upon the second and largest segment of the three—an open-deck assembly area.

The third and final section is the Shrine Room that has a wall made of Vermont marble; it inscribes all the casualties from the *Arizona*, including officers, sailors, and Marines.

The structure is 184-feet long, 36-feet wide, and 21-feet high at the ends, tapering to 27-feet wide and 14-feet high at the center. The exterior of the memorial, supported by girders, is a structure shaped like a suspension bridge. Preis's design is utilitarian and not symbolic. The dip and peak, which gave the structure proper distribution of weight, was for the support of the catenary design. The large openings were included to save as much weight as possible. Architect Preis did state his feelings and intentions of his design when he commented: "The form, wherein the structure sags in the center but stands strong and vigorous at the ends, expresses initial defeat and ultimate victory. Wide openings in walls and roof permit a flooding by sunlight and a close view of the sunken battleship eight feet below, both fore and aft. At low tide, as the sun shines upon the hull, the barnacles, which encrust it, shimmer like gold jewels ... a beautiful sarcophagus. The overall effect is one of serenity. Overtones of sadness have been omitted to permit the individual to contemplate his own personal responses... his innermost feelings." The USS *Arizona* Memorial was dedicated on Memorial Day in 1962. From that day on, the U.S.

Dedication of the new USS *Arizona* Memorial on Memorial Day 1962. More than 300 people attended the ceremony. [USAR-1715]

Navy has operated tours to the memorial. In 1980, the National Park Service, as mandated by Congress, took over operations and management of the me- morial. Alfred Preis passed away on March 29, 1993. This one structure was his crowning achievement. At his request, his ashes were spread over the *Arizona*.

The USS *Arizona* Memorial's Shrine Room with the names of 1,177 sailors and Marines killed on board the battleship on December 7, 1941.
[USS *Arizona* Memorial]

The illuminated memorial at night.
[USS *Arizona* Memorial]

The USS *Arizona* Memorial today

The new visitor center, part of the World War II Valor in the Pacific National Monument, completed in 2010.
[NPS]

The USS *Arizona* Memorial (officially the World War II Valor in the Pacific National Monument) is one of nearly 400 park sites administered by the National Park Service (NPS). This institution preserves the cultural, historic, and natural legacy of America for the education, enjoyment, and inspiration of future generations. The NPS has operated the USS *Arizona* Memorial since 1980 under a cooperative agreement with the U.S. Navy. It is responsible for the management of the memorial and shorefront visitor center, which spans eleven acres. The NPS is committed to preserving and interpreting both the tangible and intangible historical resources, and the memories, attitudes, and traditions associated with the attack on Pearl Harbor. The park is located on and adjacent to U.S. Naval Base Pearl Harbor. It consists of a visitor center, which houses several self-guided exhibits and attractions, including a museum, bookstore, a waterfront exhibit allowing visitors to visualize the events of December 7, a remembrance exhibit, and two theaters where visitors can see a documentary on the attack of Pearl Harbor. The visitor center front desk is also where visitors pick up their free tickets for the USS *Arizona* Memorial tour. The *Arizona*, which is the final resting place for the majority of the ship's 1,177 sailors and Marines who lost their lives during the Pearl Harbor attack, and the memorial is located 3/4 of a mile from the visitor center. The memorial is accessible only by boat.

Visitor Center

The shorefront area of the visitor center.
[NPS]

The visitor center is the first stop for visitors planning to tour the memorial. Located within the center are two theaters where visitors view a 23-minute documentary film on the Pearl Harbor attack prior to visiting the memorial. The museum brings visitors closer to the sights and sounds of the December 7, 1941 attack on Oahu, with personal memorabilia, dramatic photographs, artifacts of the battle, and other exhibits. Exhibits near the water's edge and the interpretive exhibit panels invite visitors to imagine the experience of that tragic day by superimposing descriptive images of Pearl Harbor as it was in 1941 across the panorama of the busy port as it appears today. Near the panels is the Remembrance Exhibit, which pays tribute to the men, women, and children, military personnel and civilians who were not on the *Arizona* that fateful morning, but whose lives were extinguished during the attack. Beyond the structural elements of the visitor center, there is a rich human subtext. Most days, one or more Pearl Harbor survivors can be found at the visitor center sharing stories and remembrances with visitors. When guests enter the visitor center, they are asked to line up for a numbered ticket, which provides free admission to the memorial tour. While waiting for the tour to begin, many visitors take a self-guided tour of the visitor center and its many attractions. When the number that appears on their ticket is called, visitors are asked to assemble at the entrance to the theaters in preparation for the tour to begin. The guided tour of the USS *Arizona* Memorial includes the documentary film depicting the attack on Pearl Harbor, a short boat trip, and a self-guided exploration of the memorial. In 1989 the *Arizona* was dedicated a National Historic Landmark.

Heather Postema, a volunteer at the World War II Valor in the Pacific National Monument, describes what this special place means to her personally:

"Turning thirty found me grateful for the all the opportunities that I had been given in my life. Therefore, I wanted to try and give back. What would be a better place than Pearl Harbor to learn some history, volunteer one's time, to be a part of all of it all? After several months of working as a volunteer, I found myself standing next to Tom Berg, a veteran from the battleship USS *Tennessee*, as he stopped beneath the flag on the USS *Arizona* Memorial and graciously shook hands with every person coming and going, easily more than 250 people thanking him for this World War service. The emotion in the air felt heavy with sadness, gratitude, respect, a great many things. We then linked arms and walked around the Memorial together, stopping for Tom to salute the flag and pay his respects. It was impossible to be in Tom's presence and not be moved. Through him it seemed one could get at least some grasp of the enormity of what had happened there on December 7, 1941.

Later, I divulged to a survivor's family member that I had felt a little sheepish being the one to walk with Tom around the Memorial as it was such an honor. She looked at me squarely and said that I was the perfect person to walk with him: "Everything that came on and after that day, all the sacrifices those men made were for *you*, just as much as everyone else, so that you could have a chance to live this life."

The people of this place have taught me that truly great men are often quite humble, instilling in one an enormous amount of reverence and respect for those who make such incredible sacrifices for the good of their country and their fellow citizens. It has shown me that I will never come close to "giving back" what has been given to me, but I still come to volunteer at Pearl Harbor to try."

Heather Postema with Pearl Harbor survivor Tom Berg.
[Courtesy of Heather Postema]

A Ranger for the USS *Arizona* Memorial

By Joey Hutton

NPS ranger Joey Hutton with his sisters Christina (left) and Theresia at the memorial. [Courtesy of Joey Hutton]

The USS *Arizona*, along with her crew, were destined to be a monumental part in American history, which is echoed in the wartime slogan "Remember Pearl Harbor". Every one of the 1.5 million visitors has their own reasons for taking the tour, and they all walk away with different feelings that is as unique as that individual.

I started my time with the USS *Arizona* Memorial (USAR) which was renamed World War II Valor in the Pacific National Monument (VALR) in 2008. It was a dream job, especially because I grew up overlooking the Memorial and Battleship Row. My grandfather, who was my hero, also worked at Pearl Harbor throughout the war, and was witness to the aftermath of the Japanese attack. My talents for understanding and interpretation of the events on December 7, 1941 made its breakthrough in 2006, when I was asked to be part of the 65th Commemoration Symposium of the attack on Pearl Harbor. That was also when my understanding about the attack on Oahu took on a new perspective. Before that experience, it was all about Pearl Harbor, and not the other military bases that were attacked that day. After the symposium, I realized the importance for tell the whole story about the attack, not just the popular story.

I gained more responsibilities as my time working at VALR went on. I began to interact with visitors in a way not many had a chance to. I became the contact and tour coordinator for the Kids Wish Network and The Sunshine Kids Foundation. It was very meaningful to be a part of their Pearl Harbor experience.

In 2008 I was chosen to be a member of a team that was responsible for researching content to be used in the new museum, which at that point was just beginning construction. That gave me access to materials that were not readily available to most of my coworkers. It also broadened my knowledge and understanding of the cultural differences between the Japanese and Americans. It is an honor to know that some of my work is on display in the museum today.

In 2008, I also accomplished something that a select and honored few have, which is to become a member of the VALR Dive Team. The feelings I had when I descended down to the *Arizona* are indescribable. It is a unique and intimate experience, especially because I was caring for the home and tomb for nearly 900 of the *Arizona's* crew. I was able to touch things that they touched, look down ladders that they used, and swim just over the decks that they walked. I had the opportunity to experience so much from my work, the most fulfilling part was the connections I made with people, including those who perished on that "Day of Infamy". Learning about the names that are etched on that marble wall on the USS *Arizona* Memorial made it even more meaningful for me to do the work that I did. There were countless Pearl Harbor survivors that I have met, along with their families. Some I still keep in touch with.

I am very grateful and honored to have had the chance to do everything I was able to do and accomplish in my time working at the USS *Arizona* Memorial. Of the thousands of people I have met from all around the world—there are two that stand out, and they are my sisters Christina and Theresia. If it were not for the events on December 7, 1941, I would have never met two of the most important people in my life.

The best way to close is in the words spoken at the end of the film before the boat ride to the Memorial: "How shall we remember them, those who died? Mourn the dead. Remember the battle. Understand the tragedy. Honor the memory."

Biography

Joey Hutton was born and raised in Aiea, a town on Oahu, Hawaii. He worked for the National Park Service at the USS *Arizona* Memorial (USAR), later designated World War II Valor in the Pacific National Monument (VALR) from 2004 to 2010. During this time, he was an interpretive ranger as well as a member of the VALR dive team.

The Museum –
Tangible Connections to the Past

The USS *Arizona* Memorial Museum is a richly hued tapestry of memories, a moving testimonial to the bravery and honor of those who served and the thousands who died in the attack on Pearl Harbor. It is an intrinsic part of the memorial experience, carrying our focus from the grand scope of a world-changing event down to the most basic level of the individuals who lived and died there. As they move through the museum, visitors are drawn into the pleasant rhythm of pre-war life at Pearl Harbor. Programs of concerts featuring the ship's award-winning big band, photographs showing sailors at work and at play, and a display case packed with trophies and victory photos can be viewed. Perhaps the most haunting of all are the letters written to the folks back home. Together they weave a visual memoir of shipboard life in a time of peace.

In stark contrast to these casual and happy mementos, there are other reminders of the catastrophic event of December 7, 1941. These include a dramatic model of the Japanese aircraft carrier *Akagi*, flagship of the deadly attack force. Another model shows the *Arizona* as she appeared before the attack. Visitors admire the proud vessel, and at the same time suddenly sense the magnitude of the destructive force that sent her to the bottom in just nine minutes. In other displays, fragments of Japanese warplanes and photos of a beached midg-et submarine carry visitors through the museum on a wave of recognition and remembrance. There is even the twisted metal remains of a Japanese torpedo that was headed toward Battleship Row before it got lodged in the harbor floor, saving perhaps hundreds of sailors from its deadly intended purpose.

This museum weaves an eloquent tale of life and death, of honor, bravery, courage, and loss. It is a wrenching human drama that holds visitors enthralled. For those too young to remember, or not yet born, the museum establishes an important link to the history of the attack. The exhibits include telegrams of condolence—small pieces of paper carefully preserved for decades by families with nothing else left to connect them to their loved ones. In another case, a row of medals gleams softly in mute testament to the bravery of a young sailor who gave his life for his country. The families of these fallen sailors have graciously donated all of these precious keepsakes to the USS *Arizona* Memorial. Pearl Harbor survivors and World War II Veterans have always played a key part in maintaining this historic site. In fact, funding for the USS *Arizona* Memorial is provided in part by the Pearl Harbor Historic Sites, a group of Pearl Harbor survivors and others interested in preserving this important legacy.

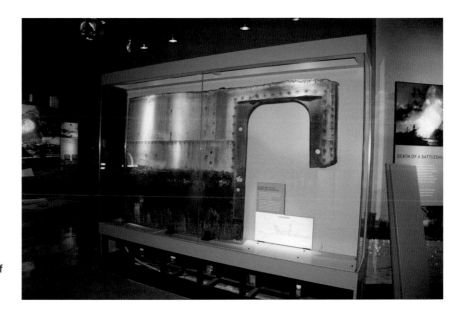

An artifact removed from the wreck of the *Arizona*.
[NPS]

DIVING INTO HISTORY
The Wreck of the USS *Arizona* today

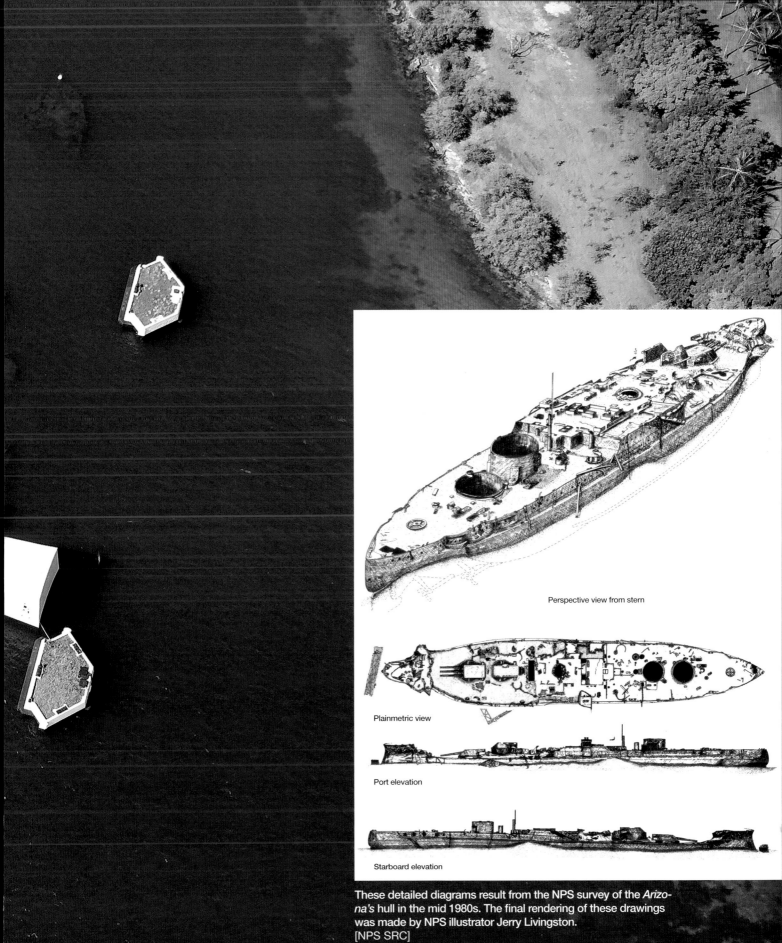

Perspective view from stern

Plainmetric view

Port elevation

Starboard elevation

These detailed diagrams result from the NPS survey of the *Arizona's* hull in the mid 1980s. The final rendering of these drawings was made by NPS illustrator Jerry Livingston.
[NPS SRC]

PLAN
Drawn in 1984

USS ARIZONA was documented during three weeks of intensive diving in 1984. Drawings were produced of a planimetric or "bird's eye" view of the ship (shown here) and of its port profile.

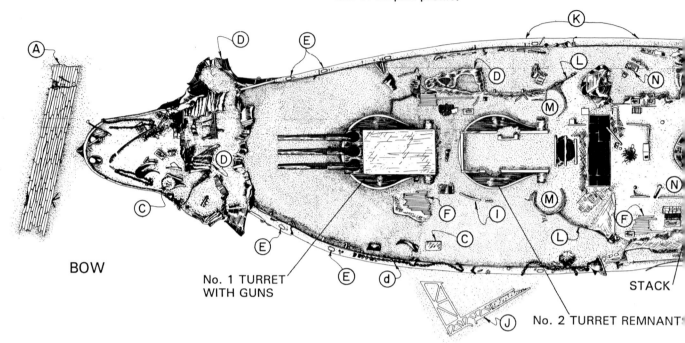

BOW

No. 1 TURRET WITH GUNS

STACK

No. 2 TURRET REMNANT

KEY

A.	CAMEL	G.	HATCH	K.	TORPEDO BLISTER
B.	CABLE RUN	H.	OPEN HATCH WITH	L.	BULKHEAD REMNA
C.	STEEL PLATE		COVER	M.	GUN TUB
D.	MISC. SHEET METAL	I	MISC. PIPE	N.	MEDICINE CABINE
E.	INSPECTION PORTS	J.	FRAME	O.	HATCH COVER
F.	TEAK DECKING VISIBLE				

WATERLINE

No. 1 TURRET WITH GUNS

No. 2 TURRET REMNANTS

OLD MOOR FOR VISITIN

FRAME

BOW

The final rendering was done by scientific illustrator Jerry Livingston, who also created two artist's perspectives of the vessel. The drawings were finalized during the winter of 1984 and released by SCRU in 1985.

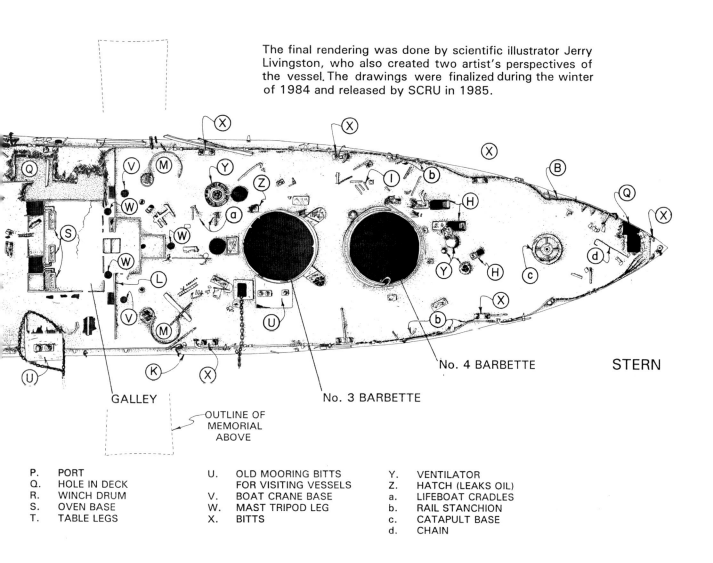

GALLEY

OUTLINE OF
MEMORIAL
ABOVE

No. 3 BARBETTE

No. 4 BARBETTE

STERN

P.	PORT	U.	OLD MOORING BITTS FOR VISITING VESSELS	
Q.	HOLE IN DECK			Y. VENTILATOR
R.	WINCH DRUM	V.	BOAT CRANE BASE	Z. HATCH (LEAKS OIL)
S.	OVEN BASE	W.	MAST TRIPOD LEG	a. LIFEBOAT CRADLES
T.	TABLE LEGS	X.	BITTS	b. RAIL STANCHION
				c. CATAPULT BASE
				d. CHAIN

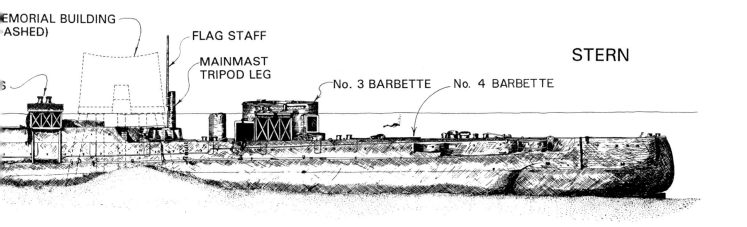

MEMORIAL BUILDING
(DASHED)

FLAG STAFF

MAINMAST
TRIPOD LEG

No. 3 BARBETTE

No. 4 BARBETTE

STERN

Exploring the *Arizona*

By Daniel J. Lenihan

▶ Watch Video:

The Science of Steward-ship

Please see instructions on page 2.

The USS *Arizona* rests heavily on the bottom of Pearl Harbor, weighted down by its own history. Seen from the bright white memorial that arches over the once proud battleship, its remains are difficult to comprehend. With the superstructure salvaged during the war and no guns visible in the wreckage, nothing suggests the remains of a great warship. A huge cylindrical Barbette on which the third turret once rotated dominates the scene. But few visitors would understand what it was without seeing the film and underwater model the park service shows them before the short boat ride. Once there, they know enough that the experience speaks for itself. It's not just what they see but being there that does it. Corroded steel from 1916 has the odor of yesteryear. It conspires with the harsh scent of oil still leaking from the ship's ruptured bunkers since 1941. It forms a thin rainbow-colored slick that is ever-present and ever moving. This unintended feature of the memorial somehow finds a place in most visitors' memories. Mixed with hushed voices, the slow shuffle of feet and distinctive headgear of park rangers, usually quiet, hands clasped behind their backs. They let *Arizona* speak for itself. No one has to be told that something important to Americans lies here. A thousand sailors, mainly young, eager, impressionable whose experience of World War II was about ten minutes long.

An archaeologist from the National Park Service dives into history.
[All photos by Brett Seymour, NPS SRC - except where noted]

The massive 14-inch barrels of gun turret No. 1. When NPS archaeologists first dove the *Arizona* in the 1980s they were surprised that this turret was still in place. Gun turrets No. 3 and No. 4 were completely removed and converted into coastal artillery batteries, while only the barrels of No. 2 were removed, with the turret itself still in place at the wreck site.

I was first shown the ship in 1982 by Gary Cummins, the memorial superintendent. Gary was deeply wedded to historic preservation and had ulterior motives for serving as my rubber-finned tour guide. He found himself the steward of a major American shrine he couldn't see–and he wanted help. As chief of the National Park Service's underwater archaeology team, I was supposed to provide such help to park managers.

Although a large white memorial spans the site, it doesn't touch the ship the only knowledge its builders needed was the ship's footprint on the bottom so they could avoid it. There were as-built plans of the ship but no maps or renderings of it since the attack. The only photographs were of the ship under way, of it being destroyed, and a few of the 1943 salvage efforts. Postcards sold in the visitor center provided

Biography

Daniel J. Lenihan has dived as a NPS underwater archaeologist since 1972. He founded a team of diving ranger/archaeologists in 1976 that in 1980 became known as the Submerged Cultural Resources Unit (SCRU). In 2000, when he retired, the team was renamed the Submerged Resources Center (SRC). Dan is the author of Submerged: *Adventures of America's Most Elite Underwater Archaeology Team*, in which he describes his many years as a Florida cave diver and chief of SCRU. He co-authored three novels with actor Gene Hackman.

The top of gun turret No.1 cannot be be seen from topside. No. 1 is the only gun turret remaining on the *Arizona*. The other three had been removed in 1942/43.

a modern aerial perspective of the ship with the memorial straddling it, but those too were deceiving. The postcards gave you a good sense of the lay of the wreck and its size. But gaping round holes left in the deck where the turrets had been salvaged reinforced common belief that the ship's 14-inch guns had all been moved to shore batteries during the war.

There was a stunning lack of facts about the remains of the vessel, which would have been unthinkable if the *Arizona* were on land.

Problems of the sort Gary was facing were the stock-in-trade of the SCRU team, as my park service underwater archaeologists are called. The Submerged Cultural Resources Unit existed to help park superintendents extend their

management skills to the underwater environment. Gary knew that he had the undocumented remains of a corroding battleship under his charge; that it contained a couple hundred thousand gallons of oil; and that some of that oil was leaking out and forming a rainbow slick on the surface. But he didn't know much more than that. By the following summer, the

SCRU team was on its way to Pearl Harbor. During our first dives to assess the ship in 1983, we swam right into the muzzles of the giant guns that weren't there. As we found in dramatic form during our first day of diving, the huge No. 1 turret is intact and in place. It can't be seen from aerial images because the forward deck has collapsed and fallen deeper. Light can't pene-

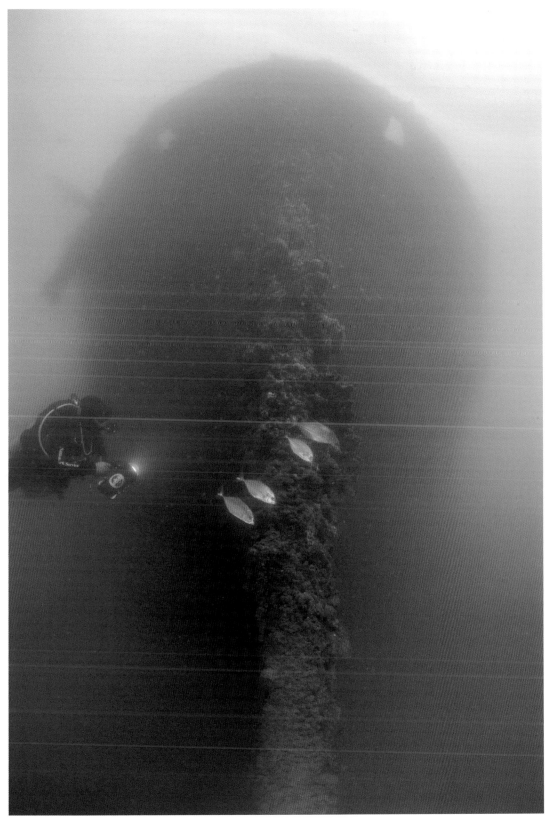

Arizona's intact bow. The NPS archaeologist provides an idea of the ship's enormous size.

An open hatch cover located on the *Arizona's* heavily damaged forward area, near to gun turret No. 2. Miraculously, this awning has remained virtually intact for over seven decades.

Arizona's intact stern. The ship's overall length is 608 feet.

trate the murky water to the new level of the turret; so, neither can sight.

We soon found there were many things on the ship that defied conventional notions and there was much to be learned. Discoveries we made each day as we mapped the ship attracted considerable attention from naval historians and the public. The *Arizona* is an incomparable touchstone to World War II. No diver stays detached for long when working on that ship. Our professional interest in measuring and mapping and recording in photography, was soon overshadowed by a personal one. By chance, just as

we began our research, the dive industry had a technological breakthrough. A way was found to replace the hopelessly awkward black-and-white video systems with newly marketed color home video cameras in underwater housings. As we began our 1983 efforts, I took a video camera down and documented what we were finding on each dive. The effect on us and on Honolulu was electric. At the end of each work session I would hand the tape cassette to a local network cameraman who dubbed the day's findings for Hawaii television. Each night, the three network affiliates aired selections from our tape. As park service researchers we work for the public and it was rewarding to see the fruits of our labor shared each evening on our hotel's TV set. Hatch-

View of the starboard side showing one of the foundation rings for the 5-inch deck guns.

Stairs that once led below decks to officers' staterooms on *Arizona's* stern now lead into sediment. Although submerged for more than six decades, these stairs still look intact.

A closed porthole in the ship's side. Some of these still contain air between their two layers of glass.

A fire hose partly buried in sediment. The *Arizona's* crew had no time to roll it out to fight the fire that would burn so many of her crew.

es looming open, porthole covers with air from 1941 trapped inside, bomb holes, live ordnance, personal artifacts-the tapes grew more compelling each day. This vicarious visual return to the war was surpassed only by the intensity of each diver's experience. For all of them, park service and navy, they were undertaking a journey into themselves as much as to the remains of a ship on the harbor bottom. They were swimming through an iconic moment in their nation's history and they knew it. Over a ten-day operation we learned what would and wouldn't work in mapping a battleship longer than two football fields, in five to seven feet of visibility. When we returned for the main project in 1984, we were ready. Pearl Harbor basks in a sea breeze most

days, zephyrs that keep the heat down and the flags high. Much of my memory of the time I spent working on the *Arizona* includes a steady sound in the background. It's the flapping of flags and pennants—"Old Glory" from the memorial, where it is still affixed to the remains of the ship's mast, and the familiar red and white of our diver-down flag. It's nice to have the familiar about you while dealing with the alien-and the texture and scent of the water around the ship was definitely alien. The odor of seawater mixed with the unmistakable aftertaste of fuel in the air expelled from our regulators. "Bunker C" is standard for a ship of this period. It oozes black, moving along the overheads at a glacial pace until it can take off toward air and light in little buoyant globules.

The *Arizona* envelops those who dive on her. You must hug the deck or some recognizable structure, or get lost. Because of the limited visibility, objects take form slowly as you swim toward them. They appear first as suggestions of a recognizable shape, then snap suddenly into a confirmation or denial of one's first impression. Regardless of the outcome, one is always surprised. Even the mundane, such as shoes, medicine bottles, chain, tile, all seem somehow special in this resting place. Strafing holes in the deck are stark and dramatic, signatures of death from above. Slivers of teak decking, intermingled with torn steel, surround larger holes made by armor-piercing bombs. The bomb-entrance holes seem small and unfathomable. Did gravity

really force them through multiple steel decks? Did a conventional explosion really convert this grand symbol of American will and might into a giant's discarded toy? The sailors are really still in there? Eventually, one's thoughts always return to the men, many of them really only boys. We know 1,177 of them perished here and have become the soul of the *Arizona*. In the end, the ship is just a ship. We glorify the feel of steel and broken artifacts, but it's the broken bodies of those boys 17, 18, 19 years old, frozen forever at those ages that tug at us when we swim by. They didn't even have the chance to be good or bad; their war lasted a little less than ten minutes. We honor our sailors and tentatively even nod to their attackers. I've seen some survivors

The *Arizona* is home to thousands of artifacts like this cooking pot.

Encounter with a seahorse. Over the years, the *Arizona* has become the home to various sea creatures.

This antiaircraft ammunition was never fired at a Japanese plane. These cartridges and numerous other artifacts are tagged with information, such as numbers, location, and condition. All tagged artifacts are cataloged enabling the NPS to monitor them over the years.

After even more than seven decades under water, the teakwood deck remains intact. Teakwood has the advantage that it does not become slippery when wet on the high seas.

of Pearl Harbor embrace their former enemies while others turn away. For the latter, the passing years have healed no wounds. Or maybe they feel it's not their place to forgive their shipmates' killers. Some wounds may be borne in peace yet never forgiven.

The two-year project that started with my snorkel-tour of the ship with Gary ended up involving us intimately with the *Arizona* for a quarter century. My sons accompanied me to O'ahu in baby strollers when we laid the first survey lines. Years later, the older dived

The memorial viewed from a diver's perspective.

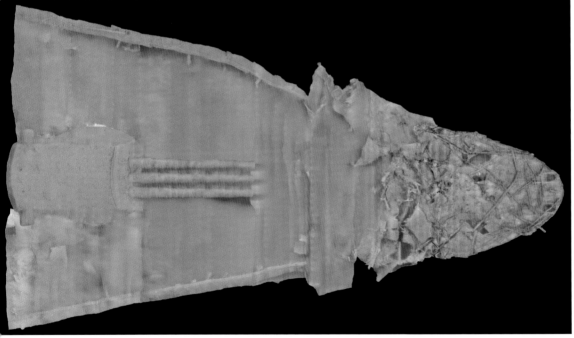

The No. 1 gun turret and the bow of the *Arizona*. In the fall of 2000, the NPS Submerged Resources Center worked with the National Geographic Society to create this photo-mosaic of *Arizona's* bow. It appeared in the June 2001 issue of the National Geographic Magazine. The crumpled bow of the sunken battleship gives evidence of the destructive force that caused the whole forward section to collapse. The murky waters of Pearl Harbor prohibit photographing such a large section of wreckage. As a result, thousands of images were stitched together creating a mosaic of the sunken bow.
[Image courtesy of National Geographic Magazine. Created by Bob Dony, University of Guelph, Ontario; Dan Nelson, TruVue Imaging; and Brett Seymour, NPS Submerged Resources Center]

the site as a member of the Submerged Resources Center, as the SCRU team was renamed. He made those dives just months before he watched the World Trade Center disintegrate on morning TV-the analogy was not lost on him. Now, both my sons are old enough themselves to serve and die. I know I would never forgive their attack-

ers, but then, one shouldn't bemoan a warrior's fate. This ship has been a great teacher for me. As a diver, I've seen many things through glass masks in very strange places. I guess all of us see through masks of some sort or another. But, my take on life, death, and calls-to-arms were all influenced by the time I served on the *Arizona*—yes, in a

peculiar way I like to think I served on her. Later than most, but also a lot longer. I've seen changes in the ship as the years have passed: survivor reunions at the 50th and 60th commemorations of the *Arizona's* sinking; personal reunions of shipmates with their ship as their urns were carried down by National Park Service or Navy divers-some I

carried down myself. I've seen fellow travelers swell with triumph, collapse in desolation, and rise again-but since my first dives on the *Arizona* I have had a place to return for renewal. It's almost like the lost sailors have gotten used to me and provide silent counsel. I anticipate their company each dive I make and on each dive, I salute them.

Imaging an Icon

By Brett Seymour

In the spring of 1998, I received a phone call from Dan Lenihan, then chief of the National Park Service Submerged Cultural Resources Unit (SCRU, later renamed the Submerged Resources Center), inviting me to join a team from the SCRU heading to Pearl Harbor. The goal of the project was to restore photo stations established by the NPS in the early 1980s on the USS *Arizona* that monitor the accumulation of marine encrustation. Kathy Billings, a new Superintendent of the USS *Arizona* Memorial believed underwater research was the key to understanding underwater sites. She also understood the importance of generating more imagery for the park's visitor education programs. I had no way of knowing that Dan's call would spark a multi decade quest to image an icon.

Early in my National Park Service (NPS) career, I never saw the *Arizona* as a stranger. Although I had yet

to visit Pearl Harbor, I had been exposed to hundreds of images in the slide files and maps that decorated the walls of the Submerged Resources Center (SRC) headquarters where I worked as a freelance photographer. I often heard Dan and former SRC Deputy Chief, Larry Murphy, speak of their work on the *Arizona* with conviction. Now I would have the opportunity to experience what they both held to be the most significant dives of their careers. As I look back, many things have changed. I am now the Deputy Chief of the SRC and with 20-plus years with the NPS I have had the honor of diving the *Arizona* more than any other in my career.

Assignments with the SRC have ranged from imaging millennia-old shipwrecks to submerged World War II era aircraft. From the first Civil War submarine, H.L. Hunley, to the last immigrant ferry, Ellis Island (to which a fourth of present-day Americans can trace their ancestry). These sites all have heritage but nothing comparable with swimming the decks of the USS *Arizona*. My dives on *Arizona* have been diverse - tending remotely operated vehicles and being a human measuring-tape weight for SRC archaeologists; supervising a Hollywood motion picture crew to producing and shooting several large

Biography

Brett Seymour is the Deputy Chief of the US National Park Service's (NPS) Submerged Resources Center (SRC) based in Denver, Colorado. The SRC supports the protection, preservation, public access, and interpretation of submerged resources, both in the United States and internationally.

Brett has been working as a full-time underwater photographer with the NPS since 1994. His work with the Service has provided underwater access to some of the United States most captivating national parks. In addition to making a whole new dimension of the Park system available to the public, for past two decades Brett has specialized in documenting historically significant underwater sites around the world.

More about the NPS Submerged Resources Center can be found at *www.nps.gov/src*. Brett's photographic work documenting the NPS's underwater realm (among other expeditions) can be found at *www.brettseymourphotography.com*

scale documentary projects. But rarely have I gotten wet without a camera. First, armed only with 36 exposures on a film-based Nikonos V—now with the latest mega pixel packed DSLR and 4K camera systems, which provide nearly unlimited images and instant gratification via LCD

monitors. With more than 500 hours underwater on *Arizona*, the single overriding goal has always been to

Right: The USS *Arizona* Memorial in rainy weather. Brett Seymour took this photograph from the ship's bow.

One of Brett Seymour's favorite photographs: sunlight touches the sunken *Arizona*.

image that tells the story is a quest—one I unknowingly began in 1998. For years I have been responding to well-meaning art directors or photo editors seeking a single photo that shows the *Arizona* resting peacefully at the bottom of Pearl Harbor. I have dreamed of what that image might be for the two past decades. My typical recommendation is an *Arizona* painting by the late Tom Freeman or the 3D digital model recently produced for the 75th anniversary—neither is constrained low visibility or air supply.

Still, I know somewhere on that ship is the next great photograph; and my quest to capture it has been the single, most rewarding aspect of my career. That quest has already led to two books highlighting the World War II touchstone. It is my hope that the image contributions to this book assist in bring *Arizona* to life for its readers—a collection of images that seeks to engage, to enlighten, and most of all to honor the USS *Arizona*. For all those who sacrificed their lives; for those few who survived and asked why; for those who come out to pay respect and perhaps most importantly for those have yet to understand and connect. Year after year the ship reveals just a bit more as I swim the decks, grateful for one more dive on *Arizona*. I try to honor the ship and those who call it theirs the best way I know how—with my camera.

create underwater imagery that reveals, inspires and honors the USS *Arizona* within the stewardship framework of the National Park Service.

The broken warship is both a dream and a night-mare assignment for an underwater shooter. The site is completely closed to any non-official diving. Even military diving is limited and closely monitored by the NPS. So, although 1,300 visitors a day view the site from above, the underwater realm of the *Arizona* is tightly controlled. But that is where the advantages end. Trying to capture a 608-foot battleship in 4 to 8-foot visibility is a challenge. Obtaining the one

A Look inside the *Arizona*

By Brett Seymour & Evan Kovacs

Because the wreck of the *Arizona* is considered a war grave, long-standing National Park Service (NPS) policy prohibits divers from entering the interior of the ship itself. In addition, the sunken battleship is a very dangerous place for even the most skilled diver. Nevertheless, full study of the site requires some means of getting inside the ship to record its condition for comparative reference in future studies.

That is where remotely operated vehicles, or ROV's, come in. ROV's have revolutionized exploration of the underwater world, because they can go where people cannot—they have become the "sharp end" of the exploration spear that can be used to scout ahead for unlimited numbers of hours before sending in dive teams for much more specialized tasks. In many cases, ROV's are used in water too deep for divers to work in safely, but they are also used in shallow water where conditions are

Watch Video:

An Interior Scientific Survey

Please see instructions on page 2.

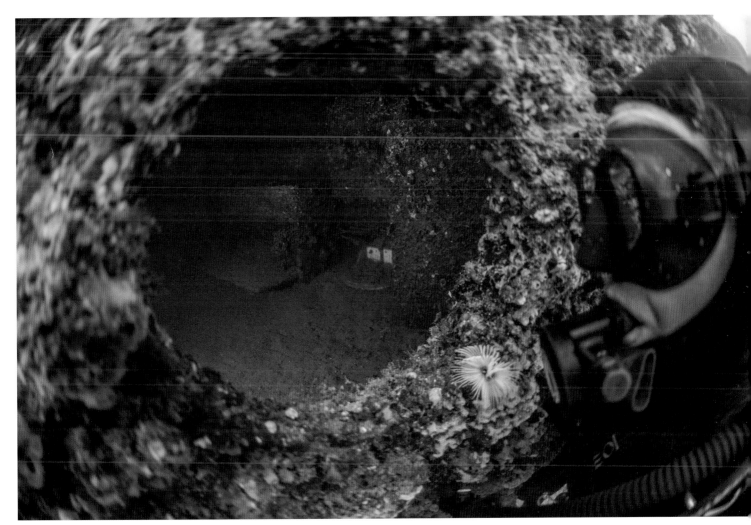

Looking through a porthole into the Marine Division Secretaries Office.

Rear Admiral Kidd's cabin. Note the remains of the table and the chair partly buried in sediment.

The ROV explores the Marine Division Secretaries Office.

too cramped, too polluted or too cold. They are also perfect for the wreck of the *Arizona*, which is structurally unstable and where researchers are intent on avoiding a human presence out of respect for the nearly 1,000 entombed sailors and marines.

ROV's have been in existence for many years, but they first caught the attention of the general public during the high profile penetration and exploration of the wreck of the *Titanic* more than thirty years ago. One of the stars of the 1985 *Titanic* documentation was *Jason Junior*, a small ROV developed at Woods Hole Oceanographic Institution (WHOI) that demonstrated to a wide audience the utility of remote vehicle technology. Jason Jr was deployed from WHOI's legendary submarine *Al-*

vin and sent back pictures from deep inside the wreck which captivated the imaginations of millions of people around the world and helped launch countless innovations for working in the deep sea.

Like most other technologies, ROV's have been made smaller, more capable, and less expensive over the last 30 years. The NPS's Submerged Resources Center (SRC) began its interior investigation on USS *Arizona* in 2000 with using a Video-Ray, an early pioneer of the micro inspection class ROV in partnership with the National Geographic Society. This early generation VideoRay weighed about 8 pounds and more importantly was small enough to fit through *Arizona* open portholes on the stern and descend below

decks via open hatches. The system was essentially a standard definition video camera with a live feed via the tether surrounded by thrusters for movement. During the expedition the NPS gained valuable insight into the interior condition of *Arizona* despite only being able to access limited areas of the second and third decks in the ships stern due to closed bulkheads or potential tether entanglements that could have resulted in a loss of the ROV. The NPS helped prove the usefulness of micro ROV's during their initial exploration of the interior of the *Arizona* more than two decades ago but since then, much has changed.

In 2016, as the 75th anniversary of Pearl Harbor approached the NPS journeyed back into the interior with a slightly larger but much more capable vehicle developed at WHOI and Marine Imaging Technologies. The vehicle carried stereoscopic 3D cameras that have over 30 times the resolution of the earlier ROV and the ability to build 3D volumetric models that scientists can use to help calculate structural integrity of the wreck. Most importantly the vehicle has a tether management system that deploys a fiber optic and copper tether from within the vehicle as opposed to pulling a tether down corridors, around corners and down stairways which is not only detrimental to the ship, but constantly hangs up the ROV. This feature alone allowed for increased range and ability within the wreck by disturbing less sediment, catching the tether less and giving scientists greater capability for scientific instrumentation.

A uniform that has survived for more than seventy years inside the *Arizona* filmed by the ROV.

The footage captured by the ROV watched by its operators.

The ROV descends through a hatch into *Arizona's* interior.

Right: The new custom-built ROV capable of capturing 3D footage in use at the *Arizona* wreck site.

The Future of the *Arizona*

By David L. Conlin, Matthew A. Russell, and Larry E. Murphy

Perhaps the nation's most hallowed war grave, the *Arizona* is slowly disintegrating, after more than seventy-five years half-buried in the bottom of Pearl Harbor. In addition to preserving this national icon for future generations, the National Park Service also is trying to prevent a potential environmental problem. Along with the remains of over 1,000 sailors and Marines, the *Arizona* still contains an estimated half-million gallons of fuel oil inside its deteriorating hull. As the battleship gradually collapses, the oil's release is inevitable. How long do we have, and is there anything we can do about it? To answer these tough questions about the ship's future, our team from the Park Service's Submerged Resources Center (SRC) has undertaken an ambitious research program to develop a long-term preservation plan for the ship.

Our research is aimed at determining the nature and rate of corrosion attacking the ship's hull. One way to understand the overall corrosion process is by analyzing scientific measurements taken systematically along the hull. These measurements help engineers and other scientists understand past, current, and possible future hull corrosion and its effect on structural integrity. At selected hull locations, Park Service archaeologists, and a diverse team of engineers, chemists, microbiologists, and other experts from

Matt Russell and Dave Conlin make notes on their slates during one of their dives.

A U.S. Navy diver uses a pneumatic drill to collect coupons of the hull and encrustation.

more than a dozen scientific institutions examined and sampled the concretion that covers the ship as well as the metal that remains underneath. Concretion, a scab of organisms and corrosion by-products that covers the vessel's exposed surfaces, holds secrets about what's going on underneath, in the steel of the ship's hull. With a pneumatic drill we bored through this encrustation (which is usually about a half inch thick), and at selected intervals inserted a small probe to measure pH and corrosion potential, a direct measure of the steel hull's active corrosion at that spot. We did this in many transects, from bow to stern, port and starboard, from the upper deck to below the point where the hull disappears into the mud. Data from these measurements are plotted, analyzed, and compared to get a better idea of how the ship is corroding, and if corrosion is uniform along the exposed hull.

Aside from the concretion covering the battleship's hull, we want to know about the steel that lies beneath since ultimately this is the main structural component of the ship. By taking a very few samples of the hull metal, and add-

ing to that metal from the superstructure of the ship that was removed during wartime salvage operations and now rests in a quiet and overgrown corner of the Pearl Harbor Naval Base, we have material that we can analyze, test and use for our computer based structural models. Not all steel is the same, and not all steel used on the *Arizona* is the same. Steel is composed primarily of iron and carbon, but adding small amounts of other materials as alloys, as well as varying the ratio of carbon to iron, results in steel with very different properties. The guns of the *Arizona* are made of one kind of steel, the decks another, the armor plating a third, the torpedo blister a fourth. In some ways *Arizona* is like a baker's cake, layered with differing recipes of steel, variations on a theme in an engineers artwork that had created a floating castle that could traverse the globe. Each of these different layers reacts slightly differently to the waters of Pearl Harbor; each of these different layers reacts slightly differently to the other layers; all of them combined create an incredibly complex puzzle of corrosion, structural strength and areas of potential weakness or collapse.

Another important part of studying the *Arizona's* corrosion is investigating

Left: Matt Russell uses a digital ultrasonic thickness gauge on the hull.

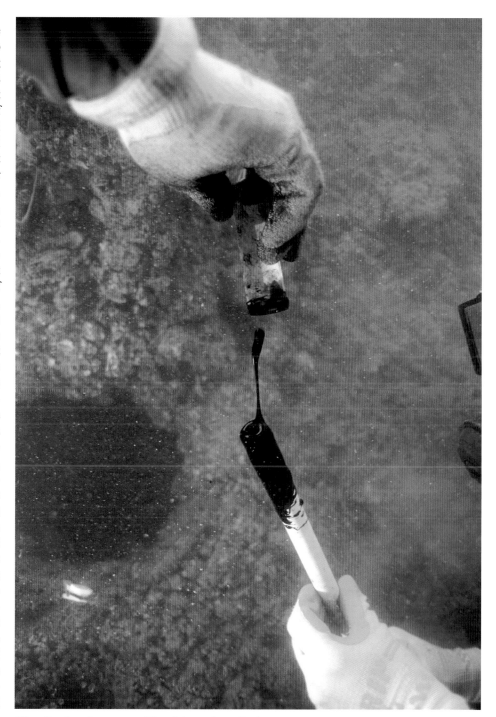

Oil collection from one of the *Arizona's* portholes.

what is happening inside the ship. The ship is not an empty shell, with corrosion happening only on visible surfaces—it is a complex three-dimensional structure with a maze of interior passageways and bulkheads that contribute to overall hull strength. Consequently, we must understand interior corrosion as well as the more easily measured exterior hull corrosion. Although we are keenly aware of the sensitivity about entering a war grave, collecting interior data is crucial to developing a realistic model of the ship's deterioration and preservation.

Because of this, and the ever-present danger posed to divers entering the vessel, we investigate interior spaces only with remotely operated technology. In our early efforts, using a miniature remotely operated vehicle (ROV), we searched for access to the ship's lower decks where the fuel bunkers are located and gathered crucial data on interior corrosion rates. Along the way we brought back remarkable images from deep inside the ship. This small ROV is about the size of a toaster, so we easily deployed it into various hatches and openings in the hull. Sitting in the control room on the Memorial above, we navigated the ROV along corroding passageways and down crumbling stairways to points deep inside the battleship where we collected a variety of scientific data, such as dissolved oxygen levels, pH, temperature, salinity, and conductivity with the ROV's onboard instruments. These parameters directly influence steel corrosion in seawater and allow us to compare interior deterioration rates to those on the outside. We also measured bulkhead thickness using an ultrasonic thickness gauge and collected samples from inside the ship for later analysis.

Ultimately, what we found is that the micro ROV was not sufficient to get us into the deepest reaches of the ship where the most important information about the condition of the fuel bunkers and corrosion is to be found. As the little robot penetrated into the interior of the *Arizona*, it dragged a cable—a tether to the surface carrying power down and video up—that dragged more and more with every corner we turned and every edge we went across. Eventually the drag of the tether was too much for the tiny motors of the submarine—we needed a better plan. A lot of late nights and more than one brainstorm later we have a better plan: a custom-built ROV from friends and colleagues at Marine Imaging Technologies and the Advanced Imaging and Visualization Laboratory at the Woods Hole Oceanographic Institution that rolls out its own tether as it penetrates into the interior ship and rolls it back up as it exits. With this new tool we were able to get deeper into the ship, get better information and gain a richer understanding of how, and why, the *Arizona* remains so remarkably preserved more than 100 years after her launching at the Brooklyn Navy Yards.

Even a ROV with a spool of its own tether doesn't get us to all the places we want to go. For the regions of the ship where we can't observe directly, we have turned to less direct ways of seeing what is going on with the ship. Oil, as it turns out, is an amazingly complex liquid that has its own story. Oil from one oilfield is chemically different from oil from another oilfield; oil that has been in contact with seawater for a long time is different from oil that has been enclosed in an oil bunker (tank), away from seawater. We are collecting oil as it is released from various locations on *Arizona*. Our questions are simple: Is all this oil from the same oil field? Has all of this oil been in contact with seawater for the same amount of time? How much chemical variation is there in the oil? Is some oil a mixture that comes from different oil fields and might be the result of refilling a half-empty tank? The answers to these questions help us understand if oil is leaking from one ruptured oil bunker or several (*Arizona* had more than 250 individual oil bunkers), if new oil bunkers are beginning to leak, or if the oil that is leaking is just an echo left over from the original attack, fuel that collected in the overheads of different compartments on the day of the attack more than 75 years ago and is only now making its way out.

The next step is to bring together the data we collected into some form that is useful for the tough decisions the Park Service and Navy managers will ultimately make. Complex computer modeling, known as a finite element modeling, is the tool we have chosen to collate all the data and to predict the most likely sequence of the battleship's deterioration. This electronic simulation, based on the best science we can collect will give managers an idea of how long we have before significant hull deterioration occurs and oil is released. The National Park Service has teamed up with metallurgists and engineers from the National Institute of Standards and Technology (NIST) in Gaithersburg, Maryland, to conduct this analysis. These NIST scientists brought experience and techniques used for analysis of the Titanic and the steel from the World Trade Center. They reconstructed the *Arizona* digitally in an incredibly powerful software package—starting with the ship as built on the day of the attack, they added the effects of the fatal blast and sixty years of immersion in salt water to bring it up to the present. Next, using data we collected on the battleship's corrosion rate, both inside and out, they are projecting the model into the future to see how quickly and in what way the ship will disintegrate. This analysis is on-going and has gotten considerably better and faster over the years we have been doing this, but the data will allow us to explore ways to slow the corrosion process and thus ensure the ship's preservation for future generations. As we gather more information, we add new details to the model, as these details change like ripples in a pond spreading outward, the models change—sometimes in ways that we could not anticipate or predict.

Inevitably, we come back to the question of oil

Matt Russell and Dave Conlin examine a sample jar of the *Arizona's* oil.

Modern laser technology used to map and visualize the *Arizona* accurately.

A coupon taken from the *Arizona* illustrates the exterior (left) and interior (right) corrosion and encrustation of the hull.

removal: should preservation of a hallowed naval tomb take precedence over a potentially invasive environmental remediation? If the *Arizona* were any other ship in any other harbor, the oil already would have been removed. The U.S. Navy and several commercial firms have the technical know-how and capability to empty sunken ships of their environmentally unfriendly fluids. This is the *Arizona* in Pearl Harbor, however, and other factors besides straightforward oil removal need to be considered. For example, although oil removal is possible, it would be an extremely destructive procedure. The *Arizona's* hundreds of fuel oil bunkers are spread across three deck levels as well as the double bottom, and arranged from bow to stern. The bunkers are highly compartmentalized, designed that way to prevent catastrophic fuel loss should one part of the battleship sustain a crippling blow in battle. Fur-

ther complicating matters, all the fuel oil storage bunkers are beneath the present harbor bottom. The ship is sunk into the sediment of Pearl Harbor to its original waterline, making direct access to the bunkers impossible.

Is this invasive and potentially damaging procedure appropriate or acceptable on these hallowed remains? Most authorities, including the Park Service, think not, at least not without considerably more information about the impact to the ship as a whole and the remains of its crew specifically. In addition to

its symbolic and historical importance, the *Arizona* also was designated a National Historic Landmark in 1989, the highest level of significance bestowed in our country. This means we need to move carefully and thoughtfully before we proceed with any remediation, and our decisions need to be based on sound scientific evidence, not pre-conceived notions or gut reactions. As stewards of the site, the Park Service is working with its many partnering scientists and the Navy to determine the best course of action. In the meantime, our efforts

are directed at discovering how long we have to make a decision and what possible options we have to slow the corrosive process so that managers can make the most informed decisions. To date the science and engineering data and modeling is telling us we have time, lots of time, several hundred years of time, to come up with the most efficient, least intrusive, and best course of action for the *Arizona* as well as the *Utah*—these historic vessels deserve nothing less.

The remains of the former battleship USS *Utah* with the memorial dedicated to her in the background. The *Utah* and the *Arizona* are the only two remaining battleships remaining in Pearl Harbor. All other battleships that were present there on December 7, 1941 have either been scrapped or sunk as targets.

Biographies

Dave Conlin is the Chief of the NPS SRC and currently the science coordinator for research on the USS *Arizona*. After an undergraduate degree in anthropology and archaeology at Reed College, Dave received a M.A. from Oxford University in Aegean and underwater archaeology followed by another M.A. and Ph.D. in anthropology and archaeology from Brown University. Following graduation, Dave took a job as an underwater archeologist with the NPS but was detailed to the U.S. Navy as their Chief Field Archaeologist. While with the Navy he helped plan and execute the recovery of the world's first successful combat submarine, the Confederate submersible H.L. *Hunley*, lost off Charleston, South Carolina, in 1864.

Larry E. Murphy retired as Chief of the NPS Submerged Resources Center in 2009 after thirty years of service. Larry began his career in archaeology in 1973 at the Florida Bureau of Archives and History and joined the NPS as one of the original members of the Submerged Cultural Resources Unit (SCRU, SRC's predecessor) in 1979. He has been director or participant in more than one hundred underwater research projects, including research at Warm Mineral Springs, the USS *Arizona* and USS *Utah*, the Civil War submarine HL *Hunley*, and in many national parks. Larry completed graduate study in anthropology at Brown University, and he has authored more than hundred publications.

Evan Kovacs has been working in the marine environment for over two decades as a diver, director of photographer and camera engineer. He has been involved in numerous expeditions utilizing remotely operated vehicles (ROVs) and submersibles to survey and film everything from the R.M.S. *Titanic* and USS *Arizona* to deep sea hydrothermal vents. Evan not only builds camera and lighting systems for these jobs through his company Marine Imaging Technologies, he is one of the few professional cinematographers qualified to use these systems at depths to 500 feet (152 meters) using scuba equipment and 14,750 feet (4,500 meters) using manned submersibles and ROVs. His underwater and topside work can be seen on National Geographic, History Channel, Discovery Channel, PBS (Emmy nominated for videography in 2009), CBC, NHK and elsewhere.

Matthew A. Russell was an archaeologist with the NPS Submerged Resources Center from 1993 to 2011. He has a B.A. in anthropology from the University of California, Santa Barbara, an M.A. in nautical archaeology from East Carolina University, and a Ph.D. from the University of California, Berkeley. As an NPS archeologist, he participated in or directed more than fort-five projects in national park areas. He was a supervisor on the HL *Hunley* Project in 2000 and was Director of the USS *Arizona* Preservation Project. Matt is currently a program manager for archaeology for Environmental Science Associates, an environmental consulting firm based in San Francisco.

SALUTE TO
A FALLEN CREW

"To the memory of the gallant men here entombed and their shipmates who gave their lives in action on December 7, 1941 on the U.S.S. Arizona."

– Inscription in the USS Arizona Memorial's Shrine Room

The USS *Coral Sea* passes the USS *Arizona* Memorial on April 18, 1963.
[Robert A. Carlisle, U.S. Navy]

Tribute to the *Arizona* and her Captain

By Charles F. Van Valkenburgh, Grandson

Chaplain Charles F. Van Valkenburgh, the grandson of the *Arizona's* last commanding officer.
[All photos Courtesy of Charles F. Van Valkenburgh - except where noted]

Captain Franklin Van Valkenburgh was one of the 1,177 men who died on board the *Arizona*.
[U.S. Naval Historical Center, NH 75840]

It was December 7, 1941; on that Sunday morning, a light breeze blew in from the west; out of the east, at just before 8 a.m., came the first flight of dark silhouettes that would mean WAR! From that moment forward, the world would join us forever in the remembrance of that awful day. A once majestic and potent manifestation of our nation's world power, the *Arizona* now lay on the bottom of the bay. Broken and burning on that day, the once powerful war machine became the eternal crypt of her mighty crew. She is not alone—our nation had suffered a devastating blow at Pearl Harbor and she is our reminder of that day and the thousands of lives that were lost. As visitors to her memorial continually remark in reverent whispers, "How she still bleeds for all those who gave their lives that day." Tiny drops of oil continuously float up to dot the waters and break silently into circular rainbows, ever expanding, until faintly blending away against the dark remains of her deck and hull a few feet under the surface of the bay.

I wasn't even born yet, but the importance of that day and that ship became as important to me as my own birthday. I have visited the memorial a number of times in my sixty-two years and I am always comforted by the serenity and respect that visitors extend to those who lay entombed below.

I want to take a moment to thank the author of this book for his extensive work. I believe that his care and attention to detail will make this a coveted addition to the literary and historical background of the *Arizona* and her crew. Mr. Bauernfeind asked me to write a few pages to be included here. When I asked what he wanted he said, "Just tell us what it was like growing up with this historical background." At first I thought it would be easy. Not so! How do you compress more than sixty years of annual funeral remembrances, "Pearl Harbor Memorial Day," into something that you can share in a book dedicated to such a grand endeavor as this. My childhood was nothing short of wondrous, but for a few bumps in the road, which I'll try to explain. I admit that the proximity of December 7 to November 30, my birthday, was, by the nature of the two events, difficult for a young child to understand. I had company though; my older brother was born on December 6 and my youngest brother on December 3. Still, when we were children, our parents went to great lengths to minimize the effects that this national and personal memorial might have on

the joy of birthday celebrations for three young boys. As I matured I developed an understanding of the importance of this day and what it meant to members of my family. As a naval officer's son, and I am the second of four, I was always exposed to the values of honor, duty, and dedication to God and country as was expected of a naval officer. Although my grandmother shared many delightful memories of life with "Daddy Van" before the war, I never recall her mentioning Pearl Harbor or the days after. I'm sure it's because it was just too much for her to relive over and over again every year!

My father, Lt. Cmdr. Franklin Butler Van Valkenburgh, was a wealth of historical and personal information and insight into my grandfather's life, and he was immensely proud of his father and of our family contribution to our country's naval history. My father served on the ship named after his father, the *Van Valkenburgh* (DD-656), a *Fletcher*-class destroyer, commissioned on August 2, 1944. The ensign hoisted upon commission that day was the same that had flown above the *Arizona's* fantail at Pearl Harbor on the morning of December 7, 1941. My father served during her commissioning and shakedown cruises as communications

Lt. Cmdr. Franklin Butler Van Valkenburgh, the son of the *Arizona's* last captain, served on board the ship named after his father, the destroyer USS *Van Valkenburgh* (DD-656).

THE WHITE HOUSE
WASHINGTON

The President of the United States takes pleasure in presenting the Congressional MEDAL OF HONOR posthumously to

CAPTAIN FRANKLIN VAN VALKENBURGH, U.S. NAVY
(DECEASED)

for service during an attack on the United States Fleet in Pearl Harbor as set forth in the following

CITATION:

"For conspicuous devotion to duty, extraordinary courage, and complete disregard of his own life, during the attack on the Fleet in Pearl Harbor, Territory of Hawaii, by Japanese forces on December 7, 1941. As Commanding Officer of the U.S.S. ARIZONA he gallantly fought his ship until the U.S.S. ARIZONA blew up from magazine explosions and a direct bomb hit on the bridge which resulted in the loss of his life."

Captain Franklin Van Valkenburgh was one of the 1,177 men who died on board the *Arizona*.
[U.S. Naval Historical Center, NH 75840]

officer. He served aboard her again during the Korean War as executive officer. As a youngster I grew up in an environment steeped in naval tradition and it seemed unlikely that I might have any other career except in the U.S. Navy. I was truly disappointed to realize that my poor eyesight, which seemed to get worse as I neared my senior year of high school, would keep me out of the Naval Academy. I did discover that I might reach my goal of a commission if I attended the California Maritime Academy, seeking a reserve commission upon graduation. I applied, was accepted, and attended my plebe year in 1964. Following a semester of academics, aboard the *Golden Bear*, training ship of the academy, we cast off on a training cruise via Hawaii to the Philippines, Hong Kong, and Yokohama before returning to San Francisco and Vallejo. When we docked in Honolulu, and I got leave, I went about making arrangements to visit the *Arizona*. It was my first time seeing her on my own, without my family, and I had no warning of the impact that this solitary ex-

perience would have on my life. I hadn't seen the memorial in the early morning light standing bright across the water, demanding respect in a solemn and quiet corner of an otherwise busy harbor. I got there early and "unannounced"—I'd been there before with the family and an entourage of VIP's and knew that wasn't what I needed. I went to

A sailor stands attention as the battleship *New Jersey* passes the USS *Arizona* Memorial.
[Rick Sforza, U.S. Navy]

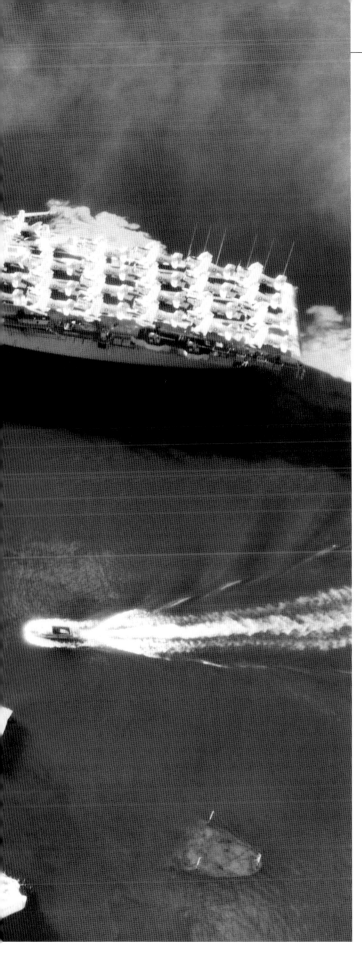

the wall and knelt quietly; some might say I was talking to God and I think they may be right, and Captain Van was on His right side, flanked by a sea of all those who gave their lives for their country. As I knelt I thought of the obligation that I had inherited, not just as the grandson of the commanding officer of the *Arizona* when she went down on December 7, but as the grandson of a man so honored by his country for his devotion to duty that he was awarded the nation's highest award, the Congressional Medal of Honor posthumously, and I was indeed humbled. I think that there must have been a seed planted that day, because I have spent many visits to the memorial since, and although each visit has its own voice, its own message, that first solo visit is sharpest and clearest to me.

I think it was the first time that I truly realized the immense burden that rested on the shoulders of those who stood before the people of my country and said, "We must go to war"! In my mind I hear repeatedly, "They shouldn't have died!" (I know I really mean Granddad!) I knew that I faced the probability of my going

The crew of the aircraft carrier USS *Bennington* spells out the name *Arizona* as the carrier passes by the temporary memorial, December 7, 1958.
[USS *Arizona* Memorial]

to war in Southeast Asia and I wondered if I would stand tall. I did serve: U.S. Army, Spec-4 Charles Van Valkenburgh, 1st Div., 1st MP Company-BIG RED ONE, Vietnam 1968–1969, and I did stand tall. I have spent the last eleven years as a member of the Veterans of Foreign Wars Silver Strand Post 5477 in Imperial Beach, California. It has also been my pleasure to serve as post chaplain for the last ten years. My community is a Navy town, on the beach, and I have had the duty and honor to chair the "Pearl Harbor Day Memorial Service" from our municipal pier each of the last ten years.

December 7, "A Day of Remembrance," that's what our [former] president [George W. Bush, in office 2001-09] called it! Officially changing "Pearl Harbor Memorial Day." The historic sixty-five-year-old event, a warning to maintain vigilance, has been reduced to a "Remembrance Day"; that had all the power and strength of a day gone by. Has this great ship and her crews, this hallowed and rusted monument, merely become an afterthought, a historical bookmark that had once been the story of the mighty battleship *Arizona*? Her memory and our battle cry, "Remember Pearl Harbor," had been a driving force behind a nation mobilized in war. I fear that we may possibly forget and the memories of those brave men and women who gave their lives might fade

One battleship salutes another. The USS *New Jersey* passes the memorial on May 24, 1986. The *New Jersey* fought in World War II, the Korean War, and Vietnam. Today she is a museum ship in Camden, New Jersey.
[PH1 Javner, U.S. Navy]

in the distance like the final notes of "Taps" floating off on a Sunday morning breeze. While kneeling on the memorial that morning I knew I had begun a life journey, a journey to honor my grandfather, a self-imposed crusade that would remain unfulfilled, perhaps even till today. "REMEMBER PEARL HARBOR" still rings in my ears and "Taps" brings tears up from my heart. Thank you all for creating this book in remembrance and may God bless these United States of America, her people, her flag, and all those who stand in her defense.

The *John C. Stennis* passes the memorial and the memorial plaque on Ford Island as the carrier arrives Pearl Harbor on July 22, 2004.
[PH1 Javner, U.S. Navy]

The attack submarine USS *Cavalla* passes the memorial on January 1, 1997.
[U.S. Navy]

Crew members of the USS *Midway* stand at attention as the carrier passes the memorial on August 23, 1991. The *Midway* fought in various wars and is now a floating museum in San Diego, California.
[Galen Walker, U.S. Navy]

Left and right: Aerial view of Pearl Harbor with the USS *Arizona* Memorial in the foreground and the USS *Missouri* in the background. Both battleships are bookends of World War II with the *Arizona* representing the initial defeat and the *Missouri* representing final victory.
[U.S. Navy]

Visiting the Memorial

Since its dedication in 1962, the USS *Arizona* Memorial has seen millions of visitors from around the world. Among them were Pearl Harbor survivors and World War II veterans with their families, American presidents, foreign leaders and dignitaries paying their tribute to the fallen sailors of the battleship *Arizona* and all the other service-men and civilians who lost their lives on December 7, 1941.

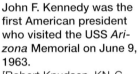

John F. Kennedy was the first American president who visited the USS *Arizona* Memorial on June 9, 1963.
[Robert Knudsen, KN-C-28995, John F. Kennedy Presidential Library and Museum]

President Kennedy in the *Arizona* Memorial's Shrine Room. The wreath serves as a tribute to the service members killed during the attack on Pearl Harbor.
[R. Knudsen, KN-C-29005, JFK Presidential Library and Museum]

President Gerald R. Ford
visits the memorial on the
35th anniversary of the
attack on Pearl Harbor, on
December 7, 1981.
[Dan R. Stanley, U.S. Navy]

Premier Zhao Ziyang of the
People's Republic of China
visits the memorial on January 7, 1984.
[Bert Mau, U.S. Navy]

President George H.W. Bush and First Lady Barbara Bush depart the memorial after their visit on December 7, 1991.
[U.S. Navy]

President Bill Clinton and First Lady Hillary Clinton during their visit on July 11, 1993.
[John Thornton, U.S. Navy]

President George W. Bush and First Lady Laura Bush with Pearl Harbor survivors at the memorial.
[USS *Arizona* Memorial]

President Barack Obama and Japan's Prime Minister Shinzo Abe present wreaths at memorial on December 27, 2016.
[M. Chu, U.S. Navy]

Arizona survivors Lauren Bruner, Glenn Lane and Edward Wentzlaff (from left to right) view the list of their perished crew members in the shrine room of the USS *Arizona* Memorial on December 2, 2008.
[Michael A. Lantron, U.S. Navy]

[Courtesy of Edward L. Wentzlaff]

There are some moments in life I do not want to remember. Then there are dastardly acts that won't let you forget ... and I consider the bombing of Pearl Harbor one of them. During three and a half years (September 24, 1938 till December 7, 1941) aboard the USS *Arizona*, I became acquainted with many of the crew members. We had great camaraderie and were very close-knit as a crew. We had respect for one another and great pride in our battleship. There are so many of my friends who were my age who died that day, and they never had the opportunity to go on with their lives. I had that opportunity and was exceptionally fortunate to experience my life and feel blessed. I have a heavy heart on each and every one of my return trips to the memorial.

— **Edward L. Wentzlaff, USS *Arizona***

[Photo by author]

[Courtesy of Glenn H. Lane]

The USS *Arizona* Memorial is a real tribute to December 7, 1941, and to our fallen shipmates who lost their lives that fateful day. It is a beautiful structure and everyone who works there seems to be truly interested in preserving the memory of the events that took place in 1941, so that those who visit in years to come will never forget the sacrifice of our men and women in the Armed Forces.

— **Glenn H. Lane, USS** *Arizona*

[Photo by author]

[Courtesy of John D. Anderson]

The attack on Pearl Harbor galvanized the United States into a strong response, in which I participated from the Artic Circle along the South Pacific Rim to the Southwest Pacific and to the Philippines for four long years of combat and three years of action in China. My brother, my friends, and my ship went down in flames. I cannot forget this and visiting the USS *Arizona* Memorial has no other feelings of what had happened.

— **John D. Anderson, USS** *Arizona*

John D. Anderson points out the name of his twin brother Delbert who perished in the *Arizona*.
[Brett Seymour, NPS SRC]

[U.S. Navy]

R. L. ALLEN	SF3c
W. C. ALLEN	EM1c
W. L. ALLEN	SK2c
J. E. ALLEY	GM1c
A. K. ALLISON	F1c
J. T. ALLISON	F1c
E. M. ALTEN	S2c
F. P. AMON	S1c
W. R. ANDERBERG	F2c
C. T. ANDERSON	CM2c
D. J. ANDERSON	BM2c
D. W. ANDERSON	SM3c
H. ANDERSON	S1c
H. T. ANDERSON	F1c
I. C. ANDERSON	MATT1c
J. P. ANDERSON, Jr.	
L. D. ANDERSON	S1c
R. A. ANDERSON	ENS
B. W. ANDREWS	GM3c
E. H. ANGLE	CCM
G. S. ANTHONY	F2c

John Anderson shows his former shipmate Donald Stratton the name of his twin brother Delbert on the wall in the USS *Arizona* Memorial's Shrine Room. Delbert Anderson was among the 1,177 crew members killed on December 7, 1941.
[Brett Seymour, NPS Submerged Resources Center]

USS *Arizona* survivor Lauren Bruner salutes his fallen shipmates.
[Brett Seymour, NPS SRC]

One Warship honors another
Tribute from the Battleship *Bismarck* Survivors

By Ingo W. Bauernfeind

On May 27, 2003, I was fortunate to participate in the 62nd commemoration ceremony of the sinking of the German battleship *Bismarck*. It was attacked and sank after one of the most dramatic sea battles in the Atlantic of World War II. During this event I had the opportunity to meet several of the *Bismarck's* survivors. One of them, Mr. Heinz Steeg, showed a lot of interest in the history of Pearl Harbor, and in particular in the *Arizona*. When I interviewed him at his home, he told me that he and his former comrades would like to donate a wreath to honor the fallen sailors of the *Arizona*. The upcoming Pearl Harbor commemoration was the 62nd anniversary on Dec. 7, 2003, and Mr. Steeg asked me if I would lay down a wreath at the memorial on behalf of the *Bismarck's* survivors.

I felt honored and responded that I would contact the historian of the USS *Arizona* Memorial, Daniel Martinez. The National Park Service welcomed this idea and suggested that I donate the wreath together with actor Ernest Borgnine. Mr. Borgnine, a World War II veteran stationed in Pearl Harbor before 1941, was the keynote speaker of the 62nd commemoration. He came to fame in the classic movie "From Here to Eternity" and later won an Oscar for his performance in "Marty". In his speech he reflected on the role of Pearl Harbor in the movies and on his own World War II experience. Dieter Heitmann, the chairman of the *Bismarck's* Survivors Association, mailed me the ribbons and I bought a wreath made in the colors of the *Bismarck's* coat of arms—blue, white, and orange. Following the official December 7 ceremony I was part of a small party taken to the memorial at around 9:00 a.m. Upon reaching the memorial, Daniel Martinez announced the *Bismarck* wreath laying ceremony as a very special honor from sailors of one of the most famous ships in history. He then introduced me as a representative of the *Bismarck's* survivors and I spoke a few words on behalf of the crew members. Daniel Martinez and the memorial's then-superintendent, Douglas Lentz, expressed their gratitude for this gesture and I laid the wreath down with Mr. Borgnine. Since there were already so many wreaths in front of the marble wall with all the names of the fallen sailors, I felt it was a special honor that Mr. Martinez allowed us to place the *Bismarck's* wreath in the center. After laying down the wreath there was a moment of silence to honor the dead. In this moment I thought about all the young men who died on these two magnificent ships and I felt that the *Arizona* and the *Bismarck* were united in honoring their fallen crews. I was grateful and felt honored that I could be part of this emotional moment. This gesture from the *Bismarck's* survivors was highly appreciated among American veterans, U.S. Navy representatives, and the general public.

Bismarck survivor Heinz Steeg had the idea to pay tribute to the *Arizona*.
[Courtesy of Josef Kaiser]

The author poses with the wreath donated by the *Bismarck* survivors. White, blue and yellow were the colors of the *Bismarck's* coat of arms.
[USS *Arizona* Memorial]

The German battleship *Bismarck* sank on May 27, 1941 with the loss of more than 2,000 lives.
[U.S. Naval Historical Center, NH 85749]

Lieutenant Zenji Abe on board the aircraft carrier *Akagi* before the attack on Pearl Harbor in December 1941.
[USS *Arizona* Memorial, USAR-2419]

Zenji Abe in later years posing in front of a restored Aichi D3A dive bomber.
[USS *Arizona* Memorial, USAR-2520]

occasions, starting with the battle on Oahu. Kaneʻohe Naval Air Station lies on the northeast shore of Oahu. In one corner of the base there stands the handsome memorial stone of Lieutenant Iida Fusata. The inscription on the monument reads, "Japanese Imperial Navy pilot—Lt. Iida Fusata—Dec. 7, 1941". The monument was built by the commander of the Third Air Traffic Control Corp. Lieutenant Iida led nine Zero fighters, attacked P-40 fighters at Bellows Field, and then proceeded north to strafe the flying boats at NAS Kaneʻohe Bay. While repeatedly attacking the base, ground fire punctured Iida's main fuel tank; in an instant, his aircraft trailed a thin white plume of gasoline. Upon noticing this, Iida gathered his men together in the air, and informed them of the compass heading and distance back to Soryu. Meanwhile, however, Lt. Iida pushed his throttle forward and charged earthward, crashing into a target. Both the aircraft and his body scattered into pieces. Naval personnel set about the grim task of providing temporary burials the next day. In a touching tribute, they gathered Iida's shattered body together and buried him with military honors, despite his status as a hated enemy warrior who had killed many of their fellow servicemen.

John Finn was in Kaneohe at that legendary moment. He showed me a small wooden box, which contained four 77-millimeter machine-gun cartridges and a fragment of aluminum aircraft skin. He saw Iida's aircraft trail gasoline while plunging toward the ground. In the aftermath of Iida's crash, he was so shocked at the tragic and gruesome scene that he nearly fainted at the sight. Finn repeated the story of Lt. Iida's sad end over and over with tears in his eyes, telling me that Americans could not conceive of such a thing. He retrieved the aircraft skin fragment and ammunition from the scattered wreckage of Iida's crashed aircraft and kept them as mementos of the Japanese pilot during the many long years since the attack. Deeply moved and touched by his words, I was at a loss for a response. Mr. Kenneth Taylor is also one of the most unforgettable people I have met. With good fortune, I had an opportunity to sit near him at the symposium in San Antonio, Texas. After an enjoyable evening playing cards and dancing, on December 7, 1941 Taylor and 1st Lt. George Welch rushed to Haleiwa Field as soon as they heard the emergency message, "Japanese airplanes are attacking Pearl Harbor." Arriving in Haleiwa, Taylor and Welch found a pair of intact P-40 fighters; they hurled themselves against the aircraft of the second wave. They were the bravest of all the pilots that day, credited with shooting down six aircraft. When I praised Taylor and Welch's bravery at the gathering, Taylor made the audience laugh by saying, "It's lucky I didn't see Abe-san then." Caught in a fight with 1st Lt. Welch over Ewa, my second man Goto's aircraft caught fire and crashed into the sea off Barbers Point.

During the fall of 1994, 53 years later, a big hurricane hit Hawaii. Soon after that a fragment of a Japanese aircraft was found on the shore at Barbers Point and it was confirmed by a military historian to be a part of Goto's aircraft. "The name of the pilot is on the fragment of the aircraft and the engine number is readable. It must be Goto's aircraft," said Mr. Daniel Martinez, the historian at the USS *Arizona* Memorial. My theme at the 50th anniversary symposium was the "Aleutian Campaign." I had become acquainted with Admiral Russell from the monu-

ment unveiling ceremony at the 40th anniversary of the Aleutian Campaign. Hearing him read my message is one of my most unforgettable memories. He was totally different from Japanese military men. He was mild, good-natured, and a sophisticated gentleman. I also had the honor of dining with Mrs. Lady Bird Johnson while I was at this symposium in Texas. Mr. Burton English, who maintained a huge ranch, invited me. Former President Johnson's ranch sat next to his, though at this time Mr. Johnson had passed away. While we were at the dinner table, Mr. English asked me, "Abe-san, please tell me if there's anything I can do for you." I replied, "I am poor and cannot afford to buy land in Tokyo but I have always wanted to be a landowner. Could you transfer me a piece of land, one square meter for ten dollars? Then, I could be a landowner, which is

my long-cherished desire." He accepted my request immediately, drew up a sales contract, and signed it. I remember Mrs. Johnson telling me, "Abe-san, I think it's a great idea. I also cannot afford to buy land in Washington. Abe-san, you have a sense of humor." I still have that contract. It is safely tucked away among pleasant memories.

Last, but not least, there is a person I will never forget as long as I live. He is Mr. Richard Fiske, who was a crew member on the West Virginia on December 7, 1941. He had thought it would be great to gather the men who bombed Pearl Harbor together with American veterans. Through Mr. John DiVirgilio, a teacher and a historian, he found a Japanese veteran who was a dive bomber pilot still living in Koganei City in Tokyo. He sent me a letter saying, "Mr. Abe, yesterday's enemy is today's friend. I don't

hate the Japanese anymore. Please come to Hawaii. We will have dinner, talk, hug, and cry together." It had been fifty years since our paths first crossed in Pearl Harbor. When we parted, I asked a favor of him, "I want to give you some money. Could you please buy two red roses every month? One for the American soldiers who died, and the other for Japanese soldiers. Then could you take the roses out to the USS *Arizona* Memorial and play 'Taps on your bugle?" He agreed, saying, "War is hell. It will be an honor to do this in memory of all those who died." He vowed to do it for as long as he lived and he kept his promise. Mr. Richard Fiske fell into eternal sleep on April 13, 2004. I will never again embrace my dearest friend Richard, nor shake his hand as we first did in December 1991 and last did in 2001.

A Nakajima B5N high-level bomber with a 1,760-lb bomb. One of these aircraft destroyed the battleship *Arizona*. [USS *Arizona* Memorial]

A SAILOR'S LIFE

By Donald G. Stratton

We got hit—it just shook the ship like it was a piece of paper. And then, just a few seconds after that, a huge explosion occurred which enveloped us.

Donald Stratton in 1942, a few months after the attack on Pearl Harbor.
[USAR-709]

My name is Donald Gay Stratton; I was on board the *Arizona* during the Japanese attack on Pearl Harbor on December 7, 1941—and survived. I was born on a farm outside Inavale, Nebraska on July 14, 1922. I went through the school system at Red Cloud, Nebraska, graduating in 1940. After being voted "The best all-around Athlete of the Year" I joined the U.S. Navy in October. I was sent to Great Lakes Naval Training Center for boot camp. After training I was at home for a week, then returned to the Great Lakes, and from there I traveled by train to Bremerton, Washington to board the *Arizona*. She was dockside being worked on by shipyard workers with electric cords laying all over the decks, welding cable likewise, air hoses and all the equipment needed to get repairs of all kinds done. We stood a lot of fire-watch on board as the welders and yard workers were working 24 hours a day.

December 7, 1941 was a Sunday morning like any other, or so we thought. We were up and around and having breakfast. I had finished eating and picked up a few extra oranges in my white hat to take to a buddy in sickbay. His name was Harl Nelson from Rouston, Arkansas—he did not survive. I went to my locker [in the bakery passageway, between No.1 and No. 2 casemates] for something; came out on deck and some sailors on the bow of the *Arizona* were shouting and pointing to some planes that were bombing Ford Island. I looked and saw the bomb blasts and thought I saw the water tower on Ford Island topple over. For some reason we recognized the planes right away as Japanese. I started immediately for my battle station. I was a sight-setter in the port AA [antiaircraft] director.

It seems that everyone has recognized what was going on and manned battle stations. Of course general quarters sounded, "THIS IS NO DRILL—man your battle stations." We were being strafed, torpedoed, dive-bombed, and hit by high altitude bombers. There was a ready box for ammunition behind every AA gun, which we started firing immediately at dive bombers and later at the high altitude bombers, which our shells never reached, as we could see the bursts very short of targets. Running short on ammunition, Ensign Lomax, our director officer, went to see if he could speed up the ammunition supply, but I never saw him again. He did not survive. About that time we were hit with something that shook the ship very badly—it could have been the 2,000-lb bomb that hit starboard right aft to No. 2 turret, or it could have been a torpedo—as I saw from my vantage point two torpedo wakes headed right for the *Arizona*. Only the good Lord knows where they wound up.

Then: the horrendous explosion that blew about 110 feet of the bow off, with a fireball that went 400 to 500 feet in the air and engulfed the whole forward half of the ship. The explosion following the bomb hit was caused by ammunition powder, aviation gasoline (180,000 gallons), and, of course, fuel oil. What an awful, horrendous day this was, watching sailors and Marines fight for this wonderful country and fight for their very lives (with so many perished). Some below decks did not know what hit them. The worst tragedy, of course—the young American lives lost. But did we learn anything? Let us keep America alert, for they say history has a way of repeating itself. I guess being inside the director saved some of our lives on the sky control platform, as I recall it took forty to fifty men to man both port and starboard sides of the sky control, ten men to each director, plus all the observation personnel and plane spotters. I do not know what happened to most of them, as only six of us went across a line to the

repair ship *Vestal*. She was tied up outboard of us as they were doing some work on the *Arizona*. We could not go down the ladders as everything was burning. As the flames died down we were out on the platform with nowhere to go. There was a sailor (Joe George, I found out later) out on the afterdeck of the Vestal who threw us a heaving line and attached a heavier line, which we pulled across to the *Arizona* and tied to the sky control platform, then proceeded to go across the line hand over hand, after we were burned very badly. Six of us went across that line and I think there are only two of us alive, Lauren Bruner and myself.

I was burned over sixty-five percent of my body. It also was about 45 feet up, over a lot of fire and water. After we were aboard the *Vestal* for a while we were put on a motor launch and taken to the landing where we were loaded on an open-air truck and driven to the U.S. Naval Hospital in Pearl Harbor. I was there for a few days and they decided to send some of us back to the mainland. Of course I wanted to go, but they didn't know if I would make it or not, so they decided if I could get up and stand by the side of my bed while they changed the linens, then I could go.

Donald Stratton visits the USS *Arizona* Memorial during the 75th anniversary of the attack on Pearl Harbor, 2017. [Brett Seymour, NPS Submerged Resources Center]

Donald Stratton's battle station was the antiaircraft (AA) director on the portside of the sky control platform. From here, he and five shipmates went across a line to the repair ship *Vestal* which was moored next to the *Arizona*. [USS *Arizona* Memorial]

I did so, but when I laid back down I did not get up for a very long time. I arrived aboard a ship named *Scott* at Mare Island Naval Hospital on Christmas Day, 1941. It is needless to say, I have a soft spot in my heart for all the doctors, nurses, and corpsmen of the U.S. Navy. After several months of a lot of saltwater baths and a lot of healing, I was transferred to Corona, California for a convalescence period. I was medically discharged on September 1942, as my left arm and leg were not too good yet. I went back to Red Cloud,

Nebraska, where I did different jobs for a while. I went through the process of getting back in the U.S. Navy with the help of my draft board. I was held up in Omaha, Nebraska for a few days while they got clearance from the Navy. I got my same service number, which helped a lot in the years to come. I had to go back through boot camp again, in Farragut, Idaho as recruit CPO. I could have stayed there but I wanted to go to sea, so I was sent to Treasure Island where I boarded the destroyer *Stack*, which proceeded to

the South Seas. This was all in 1944. We were in all the invasions through New Guinea, Halamahera, Leyte, and Luzon, also Okinawa. I was transferred to electric hydraulic school in San Diego, California, then sent to St. Louis, Missouri, and discharged, this second time as a gunner's mate 2nd class (GM 2c) on December 4, 1945. I returned to Red Cloud, Nebraska where I met and married Velma Lockhart in 1950. To our household we added first our son Robert, now of Santa Barbara, California and a Vietnam veteran. Then Gypsy Dawn, who survived only three days; then Randy, now in Colorado Springs, Colorado, then Roxanne Jo, who survived only five days. I guess the good Lord has his own way of doing things, for now we have four wonderful granddaughters and one grandson, one great-grandson, and one deceased great-grandson. One granddaughter graduated three years ago from Baylor University and now coaches the women's basketball team of UCCS in Colorado Springs, and the sister is going to be a senior at Washington State play-

ing basketball. The other two granddaughters are both working and living in California. The grandson was signed 13th overall and first-round draft pick by the New York Mets in 1996. He is now with the New York Yankees. I went to work on offshore drilling barges as able-seaman and as a barge master. Later I went to work with deep-sea divers as a diver-tender. I worked all over the world: Alaska, Columbia, Chile, Kuwait, Nicaragua, as well as in the United States. A lot of pipeline work and erecting offshore drilling platforms. I made a dive in a two-man submarine well over 1,100 feet.

In 1986 I retired and moved to Yuma, Arizona, where we lived for fifteen years, then finally moved back to California. Now we live in Santa Maria. Our flag, duty, honor, courage, and the people who made the supreme sacrifices for our freedom, shall always be remembered. Keep America alert, so that something like this does not happen again, or else all those sacrifices were for naught.

"God Bless America."

Donald Stratton with his family during a visit to the USS *Arizona* Memorial.
[Nikki Stratton]

ARIZONA AS A MODEL

By William J. Blackmore

My model of the Arizona is an ambassador of American history that other people can see, touch, and interact with—bridging the gap between factual events and the current generation.

When I was six years old, the movie *"Tora, Tora, Tora"* came out, and I remember going to see it with my parents. From the opening frames of the attack on Pearl Harbor I was hooked on the story of that attack, and specifically, upon the ships of the Pacific Fleet. Not long after seeing the movie for the first time I found a plastic model of the U.S.S. *Arizona*, which I bought after the kit's box art drew my gaze. The images of the crew defending their ship instantly sent my mind back to the movie, which had so profoundly imprinted itself into my imagination.

As a young adult, I began building models on commission almost by accident. When I approached the Patriot's Point Naval Museum in Charleston, South Carolina, about the possibility of building a model for them, I was given a list of subjects to choose from. At the very top of the page the name *"Arizona"* jumped out at me. I departed the museum with the commission to build a large-scale model of the ship whose design I had come to love so much.

Sometime during the process of building the model I learned of a number of people that had enjoyed building radio controlled scale model ships. I promised myself that if I ever had the opportunity to build a model like that, I would do it.

In the years following my first *Arizona* project, I began learning about radio controlled ship models and some problems associated with running them. One of the main considerations of R/C model warships—just like real ones—can be that they are very hard to see at distances beyond thirty yards or so, especially if the model builder applies a realistic finish to the model. When I built my model of the *Arizona* I thought about the model's final appearance and decided that I truly liked the ship's final overall design, but I did not like the paint scheme. I also reasoned that applying the Measure One camouflage, like the original *Arizona* used at Pearl Harbor, would work a little too well whenever I tried to run the model on the dark waters of a pond. Finally, I considered that I favored

William Blackmore's model ready to go to sea.
[William J. Blackmore]

The original *Arizona* during the 1930s (large picture). The model of the *Arizona* photographed from the same angle as the original ship. [USAR-443]
Inset: William Blackmore's *Arizona* model. [W. Blackmore]

the older design of the SOC Seagull biplanes more than the OS-2 Kingfishers the real ship carried at the end of her life, so my problem was how to combine all the elements that I liked with historical fact without violating my own dedication to realism.

While looking through Paul Stillwell's book *"Battleship Arizona"* I found a picture of the ship at Puget Sound in January 1941 that showed the ship still wearing her peacetime light gray paint. A little further research showed that

I could also use the SOC Seagull aircraft and still be true to accuracy. My course was set, and I proceeded with construction.

I started building the *Arizona* on a commercially available fiberglass hull, which I reinforced with a plywood bottom and ribs. I built a watertight box into the bottom of the hull for the radio equipment and wired the interior with lighting to allow maintenance. I built and tested many of the items that animate the model's various functions on my desk and

installed them into the hull. I completed extensive testing of the model's rotating gun turrets, working main boat cranes, fire control system, independent throttle controls, rudder, bilge pumps, and fully functional anchor, and installed them into the hull.

I built the superstructure, stack, and main tripod mast from styrene plastic. The barbettes were made from PVC pipe; the guns turned from brass, and the turret housings from fiberglass. I used commercially available fittings, including all

the 5"/51 and 5"/25 guns. A friend of mine provided me a large sheet of photo-etched parts in 1/96th scale that he generously enlarged from a smaller scale kit of the *Arizona* that he had produced. This photo-etched brass included the aircraft crane, catapults, large cranes, and outriggers attached to the rear of the forward fighting top. With all this detail to contend with, the most difficult problem proved to be figuring out how to access the interior equipment and batteries. The solution was to remove the entire forward part of the superstructure up to the number two barbette. Just before the model's official launching, I installed a glass tube of soil from the State of *Arizona* sent to me by a friend in Phoenix, and a limited edition "Day of Infamy" coin.

Moving the model out to a lake to "get 'er wet" is always a logistical nightmare. Every move must be known and practiced before actually doing anything to avoid damage. Keeping the curious at a safe distance, answering the flurry of questions that always follow, while coincidentally handling the 125 pound behemoth without stumbling, bumping something fragile, or getting snagged on one of the myriad protrusions must be something akin to juggling wild ferrets on a high wire running through a forest. To solve these problems, I built a wheeled transportation dock to get the model from our van to the water's edge. Once the transportation dock is in place, I roll the entire affair into the water just like launching a bass boat.

Actually running the model requires almost as much care and forethought as its transportation to the lake it patrols. Like the real *Arizona*, the model handles quite well in open water, is stable because of the rather flat bottom, but slow in turning, and hard to control at slower speeds. Knowledge of the waters it roams is essential to avoid running

aground or entanglement in fishing lines or other obstacles. My decision to finish the model in *Arizona's* January 1941 arrangement not only provides hours of stunning visual excitement, but also allows far greater confidence in her control at longer distances. Video equipment records every trip to the lake just in case the worst happens. Aside from providing a clue to the model's potential resting place, it might provide some rather "cool" footage of the disaster. In all cases the *Arizona* draws attention wherever she goes.

As the day passes I often find myself teaching an impromptu history lesson at the water's edge. People study the details of the model closely, ask questions, and often lose themselves in the moment watching the model pass serenely over the water. Before they know it, observers of all ages either learn something important about our nation's history, or remember quietly about a day long ago, now so disconnected from present reality, always seen in the gray tones of black and white film. Their reflections remind me that my model is more than just a big toy, or a very expensive past-time.

In a small way that I never foresaw, my model of the *Arizona* is an ambassador of American history that other people can see, touch, and interact with— bridging the gap between factual events and the current generation. A manifest

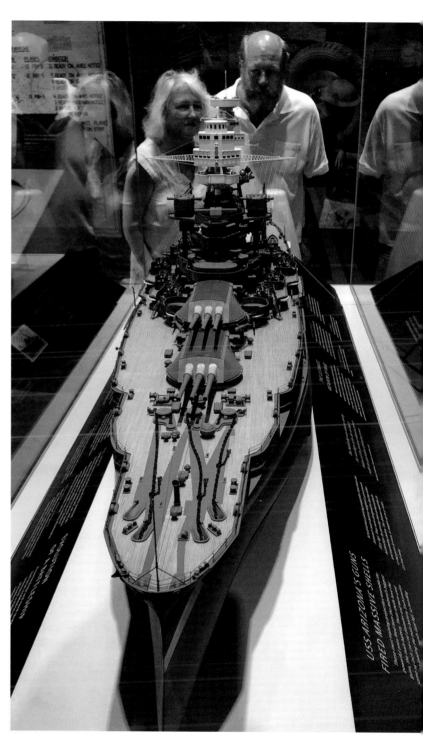

Another model of the *Arizona* on display at the visitor center in Pearl Harbor.
[Burl Burlingame]

representation that gently cajoles the observer to remember that day so long ago, and perhaps, think

about the meaning of sacrifices made by so many for generations never known to them.

COMMEMORATING THE *ARIZONA*

The Great Gathering:
The Pearl Harbor 50th Anniversary

President George H. W. Bush was the keynote speaker at the 50th Pearl Harbor Anniversary.
[US Dept. of Defense]

Medal of Honor recipient Donald K. Ross helped to keep the battleship *Nevada* operational during the attack on Pearl Harbor.
[U.S. Navy]

The 50th anniversary of the attack on Pearl Harbor which took place on December 7, 1991 saw the largest gathering of Pearl Harbor survivors commemorating the tragic event that ended more than 2,000 lives prematurely and propelled the United States into World War II. Keynote speaker on this very special day was President George H.W. Bush, a naval aviator during the fighting in the Pacific. He was introduced by Captain Donald K. Ross (U.S. Navy, ret.), a surviving crew member of the battleship USS *Nevada* and recipient of the Congressional Medal of Honor. After thanking him for the introduction, President Bush delivered his remarks:

"It was a bright Sunday morning. Thousands of troops slept soundly in their bunks. Some who were awake looked out and savored the still and tranquil harbor. And on the stern of the USS *Nevada*, a brass band prepared to play "The Star Spangled Banner." On other ships, sailors readied for the 8 a.m. flag raising. Ray Emory, who was on the cruiser *Honolu-*

lu, read the morning newspaper. Aboard *California*, yeoman Durell Connor wrapped Christmas presents. On the *West Virginia*, a machinist's mate looked at the photos just received from his wife showing his 8-month-old son whom he had never seen. On the mainland, people listened to the football games on the radio, turned to songs like the "Chattanooga Choo-Choo," comics like "Terry and the Pirates," movies like "Sergeant York." In New York, families went window-shopping. Out West, it was late morning, many families still at church. At first, to the American sailors at Pearl Harbor, the hum of engines sounded routine—and why not? To them, the idea of war seemed palpable but remote. And then, in one horrible instant, they froze in disbelief. The abstract threat was suddenly real.

But these men did not panic. They raced to their stations, and some strapped pistols over pajamas, and fought and died. And what lived was the shock wave that soon swept across America, forever immor-

talizing December 7, 1941. Ask anyone who endured that awful Sunday. Each felt like the writer who observed: "Life is never again as it was before anyone you love has died; never so innocent, never so gentle, never so pliant to your will."

Today we honor those who gave their lives at this place, half a century ago. Their names were Bertie and Gomez and Dougherty and Granger. And they came from Idaho and Mississippi, the sweeping farmland of Ohio. And they were of all races and colors, native-born and foreign-born. And most of all, of course, they were Americans. Think of how it was for these heroes of the Harbor, men who were also husbands, fathers, brothers, sons. Imagine the chaos of guns and smoke, flaming water, and ghastly carnage. Two thousand, four hundred and three Americans gave their lives. But in this haunting place, they live forever in our memory, reminding us gently, selflessly, like chimes in the distant night.

We remember machinist's mate Robert Scott who

ran the air compressors powering the guns on board *California*. And when the compartment flooded, the crew evacuated; Scott refused. "This is my station," he said, "I'm going to stay as long as the guns are going." And nearby, aboard the cruiser *New Orleans*, Chaplain Forgy assured his troops it was all right to miss church that day. His words became legend: "You can praise the Lord and pass the ammunition."

Captain Ross, right here, was awarded the Congressional Medal of Honor for his heroism aboard the *Nevada* that day. I salute him and the other Congressional Medal winners with us today, wherever they may be also. For the defenders of Pearl Harbor, heroism came as naturally as breath. They reacted instinctively by rushing to their posts. They knew as well that our Nation would be sustained by the nobility of its cause.

So did Americans of Japanese ancestry who came by the hundreds to give wounded Americans blood, and the thousands of their kinsmen all across America who took up arms for their country. Every American believed in the cause. The men I speak of would be embarrassed to be called heroes. Instead, they would tell you, probably with defiance: "Foes can sink American ships, but not the American spirit. They may kill us, but never the ideals that made us proud to serve."

Back in 1942, I remember how Henry Stimson,

the Secretary of War, defined the American soldier, and how that soldier should be, and I quote: "Brave without being brutal, self-confident without boasting, being part of an irresistible might without losing faith in individual liberty." The heroes of the Harbor engraved that passage on every heart and soul. They fought for a world of peace, not war, where children's dreams speak more loudly than the brashest tyrant's guns. Because of them, the USS *Arizona* Memorial lives to pass its lessons from one generation to the next, lessons as clear as this Pacific sky. One of Pearl Harbor's lessons is that together we could "summon lightness against the dark"—that was Dwight Eisenhower. Another, that when it comes to national defense, finishing second means finishing last.

World War II also taught us that isolationism is a bankrupt notion. The world does not stop at our water's edge. And perhaps above all, that real peace, real peace, the peace that lasts, means the triumph of freedom, not merely the absence of war. And as we look down at—Barbara and I just did—at *Arizona's* sunken hull, tomb to more than 1,000 Americans, the beguiling calm comforts us, reminds us of the might of ideals that inspire boys to die as men. Everyone who aches at their sacrifice knows America must be forever vigilant. And Americans must always re-

31 *Arizona* survivors rise to receive the audience's applause during the 50th anniversary of the attack on Pearl Harbor. [Terry Mitchell, U.S. Navy]

member the brave and the innocent who gave their lives to keep us free.

In Pearl Harbor's wake, we won the war and, thus, the peace. In the Cold War that followed, Americans also shed their blood, but we used other means as well. For nearly half a century, patience, foresight, personal diplomacy helped America stand fast and firm for democracy. But we've never stood alone. Beside us stood nations committed to democracy and free markets and free expression and freedom of worship, nations that include our former enemies—Germany, Italy, and Japan. This year these same nations stood with us against aggression in the Persian Gulf.

The war in the Gulf was so different: we fought a different enemy and did this under different circumstances—the outcome

A survivor from the battleship *Nevada* commemorates his fallen shipmates. [U.S. Navy]

The USS *Missouri* pays tribute to the sunken *Arizona*. In 1991, the *Missouri* was the world's last active battleship. [U.S. Navy]

never in doubt. It was short; thank God our casualties mercifully few. But I ask you veterans of Pearl Harbor and all Americans who remember the unity of purpose that followed that momentous December day fifty years ago: Didn't we see that same strength of national spirit when we launched *Operation Desert Storm*?

The answer is a resounding "yes." Once the war for Kuwait began, we pulled together. We were united, determined, and we were confident. And when it was over, we rejoiced in exactly the same way that we did in 1945—heads high, proud, and grateful. And what a feeling.

Fifty years had passed, but, let me tell you, the American spirit is as young and fresh as ever.

This unity of purpose continues to inspire us in the cause of peace among nations. In their own way, amidst the bedlam and the anguish of that awful day, the men of Pearl Harbor served that noble cause, honored it. They knew the things worth living for but also worth dying for: Principle, decency, fidelity, honor. And so, look behind you at Battleship Row— behind me, the gun turret still visible, and the flag flying proudly from a truly blessed shrine. Look into your hearts and minds: You will see boys who this day became men and men who became heroes.

Look at the water here, clear and quiet, bidding us to sum up and remember. One day, in what now seems another lifetime, it wrapped its arms around the finest sons any nation could ever have, and it carried them to a better world.

May God bless them. And may God bless America, the most wondrous land on Earth."

From Memory to History?
The Pearl Harbor 75th Anniversary
By Geoffrey White, Ph.D., and Daniel A. Martinez

If 50th anniversaries of war tend to be the last grand occasion in which the war generation's veterans and survivors commemorate their war, what do 75th anniversaries do? And for whom? Whereas the 50th anniversary of the Pearl Harbor attack in 1991 ushered in a period of national commemorations featuring veterans billed as the Greatest Generation who fought America's Good War, what will the 75th anniversary feature?

For Americans born after the war the 75th anniversary on December 7 marks the turn toward an era of post-witness remembrance. Yes, a handful of veterans will attend ceremonies at Pearl Harbor, but stories appearing during the run-up to the anniversary focus as much on the passing of survivors as on their stories. Most recently the death of Raymond Haerry, one of only six remaining survivors from the battleship USS *Arizona*, made national news.

Although it is foolish to set the words 'memory' and 'history' in opposition to one another, the end of the era of first-person witnessing for World War II, so often discussed in the literature on the Holocaust, sees history supplanting (and appropriating) memory, at least if we think of the latter as rooted in spoken narrative. What might this mean for commemoration of the Pearl Harbor 75th? The most visible change, it seems, is not so much a move away from storytelling as an expansion of the range of stories deemed relevant for commemoration. While Pearl Harbor will always be a place where martial narratives of heroism and sacrifice find a prominent stage, the current moment suggests a greater tolerance for less narrowly patriotic analyses of the politics and conduct of the war.

If changes at the national Pearl Harbor memorial in Hawaii are any indication, the 75th anniversary will reflect an ongoing shift away from a historiography centered only on the stories of American combatants to a broader canvas of conflicts that also in-

Jacqueline Ashwell, the VALR's superintendent, speaks at the 75th Pearl Harbor anniversary. [Brett Seymour, NPS SRC]

cludes homeland sacrifices and injustices as well as the perspectives of former enemies and themes of reconciliation. The fact that the USS *Arizona* Memorial is a burial place ensures that remembrance there will always to some degree be predicated on narratives of death and sacrifice, inscribed in a memorial wall of names and personalized in the stories of medal recipients. And yet the past ten years of commemoration at Pearl Harbor have shown a progressive expansion of official history to encompass such subjects as the experiences of civilians, Japanese American internment, and Japanese perspectives on the war. Still mostly in the margins, however, and in many

Arizona survivor Donald Stratton and historian Daniel Martinez salute during the 75th anniversary. [Brett Seymour, NPS SRC]

Arizona survivor Louis Conter poses for a photo with visitors.
[Brett Seymour, NPS SRC]

or excluded from official memorial space began to take their place alongside military remembrance. These included a Japanese tea ceremony conducted on the memorial in 2011 and a permanent museum exhibit about an iconic atomic bomb victim (Sadako Sadaki, a 12-year-old girl who succumbed to radiation sickness) dedicated in 2013. Neither of these events would have been considered during the 1980s and 90s when Japanese participation was pointedly excluded from official events in the sacred centers of national memory. During the last decade, however, as United States strategic interests in the Pacific have increasingly looked to Japan to expand its military capacity, the U.S. Navy has shown greater interest in the co-sponsorship of commemorative activities. Indicative of the embrace of relations with Japan in recent commemorative activities, the official theme of last year's 74th anniversary of Pearl Harbor was "Pathway to Reconciliation: From Engagement to Peace."

Although less of a hot button issue than Japanese presence in memorial events, Japanese American issues and perspectives also remained in the margins of Pearl Harbor commemorative activities through much of the twentieth century. Thus, the National Park Service documentary shown to all those who visit the USS *Arizona* Memorial could refer to

base commanders' worries about Japanese American sabotage without making reference to the actual state of Japanese American loyalty or the post-attack detention of large numbers of Japanese residents, American citizens and immigrants alike. With growing public recognition of the injustices of internment as well as the distinguished military service of Japanese Americans, Japanese American issues have taken a more central place in Pearl Harbor exhibits and anniversaries. The current issue of the magazine *Remembrance*, put out by the nonprofit partner of the National Park Service at Pearl Harbor, is dedicated to the stories of Americans of Japanese ancestry, introduced by pointing out that, "…it was not just an attack on Pearl Harbor. The human story goes beyond the brave men in uniform that day… There is also an Oahu story that includes American citizens of Japanese ancestry who suffered untold hardship and would end up in a war fought on two fronts." And the creation of a new national monument at the site of the largest internment camp in Hawaii, Honouliuli—a site that confined both Japanese Americans and Japanese military prisoners of war in the same facility—ensures that the "tell the history of internment, martial law, and the experience of prisoners of war in Hawaii during World War II" will join the Pearl Harbor attack in the ways World War II

ways silenced by the call to remember, are the voices of Native Hawaiians, many of whom regard the U.S. naval base at Pearl Harbor as a painful symbol of military occupation and loss.

Following the creation of a new national monument in 2008 that grouped the USS *Arizona* Memorial together with several other World War II sites (the World War II Valor in the Pacific National Monument) and the opening of a larger museum and visitor center at Pearl Harbor in 2010, events that would have once been marginal

The memorial in the early morning hours before a floral tribute that followed the 75th anniversary ceremony.
[Katarzyna Kobiljak, U.S. Navy]

is remembered in national historic sites.

This year's anniversary offers a public demonstration of these emergent transformations in the official centers of national memory. Certainly military ceremonies with honor guards, speeches and wreath presentations will continue to occupy center stage. At the same time, however, the lineup of official events scheduled over the course of eleven days offers up a highly varied set of activities. To some extent the anniversary program has the feel of a festival complete with band performances, film showings, gala fundraisers and even a "Fox Sports Pearl Harbor Basketball Invitational." And yet specific commemorative activities include a tribute to Japanese American veterans

titled "Fighting Two Wars," two events honoring Doris Miller, the most well-known African American sailor decorated for his actions during the attack, and two "private events" involving Japanese nationals making offerings on the USS *Arizona* Memorial. The latter include a presentation titled the "Blackened Canteen Ceremony" that features a Japanese citizen honoring an American bomber crew who perished in a bombing raid on his hometown and a second, labeled an "Interfaith Prayer Service," that brings together "diverse spiritual leaders," including several Japanese Buddhist organizations, to offer prayers for "all of those that gave their lives on that fateful December day representing veterans of the United States and Japan."

Historically, Americans alive in 1941 needed no explanation of the importance of the Pearl Harbor bombing. Those born after the war, if they know it at all however, may know it only as a mythic moment in the timeless past. Postwar generations have their own critical events that define turning points in their lives. Thus, the September 11 attacks that were instantly compared to the Pearl Harbor bombing

when they happened now supplant them in American historical consciousness. If the Pearl Harbor bombing is still, in some quarters, invoked to understand the September 11 attacks, in what ways might the history of the remembrance of Pearl Harbor inform the ways Americans remember September 11? Is it possible that an iconic call to "remember" in one era actually becomes a vehicle for forgetting in another?

Biography

Geoffrey White, Ph.D., is professor emeritus in the department of anthropology at the University of Hawaii. His book *Memorializing Pearl Harbor: Unfinished Histories and the Work of Remembrance* was published Duke University Press in 2016.

MEMORIAL, MYTH, AND SYMBOL

By Dr. James P. Delgado

"The Arizona's loss serves as a vehicle for personal reflection on the causes, conduct, and result of war."

[Courtesy of James P. Delgado]

While the archaeological evaluation of the attack on Pearl Harbor fascinates many Americans, it is the event itself that so ingrained itself in the nation's consciousness. Pearl Harbor, particularly the *Arizona*, has become a national shrine. Pearl Harbor and every trace of the American forces that defended it are now imbued with an almost religious significance. As such, the *Arizona* and the *Utah*, along with pieces of other battleships are relics of considerable cultural value, while artifacts associated with the attacker have their own special emotion-al impact for citizens of both nations. The *Arizona* and the USS *Arizona* Memorial have become a major shrine and point of remembrance, not only for the lost battleship but also for the entire attack. The explosion that destroyed the *Arizona* shook the harbor, blowing debris and parts of bodies for thousands of feet. It was the central event of the attack and remains central in the reminiscences of most survivors. Indelibly impressed into the national memory, the USS *Arizona* Memorial is visited by millions who quietly file through, toss flower wreaths and leis into the water, look at the rusting hulk through the oil-stained water, and read the names of the dead carved on the marble plaque attached to the memorial's walls—perhaps more important than the modern memorial that straddles it is the battleship itself, which is the ultimate shrine. Resting in the silt of Pearl Harbor, the *Arizona* is a naval memorial and a war grave. It was the scene of tragedy, triumph, and heroism. The wreck is also a crystallized moment in time, its death wounds visible and still bleeding oil, the intact hull holding most of the crew.

The *Arizona* as a Naval Memorial

The concept of naval memorials is an ancient one. Naval memorials can be prizes of war: the flags, weapons, or vessels of the enemy. War prizes, for the most part, have focused on the preservation of vessels as trophies. Octavian, following his victory over Antony and Cleopatra's fleet at Actium, erected a memorial on the hill overlooking the battle site adorned with the bronze rams from the prows of dozens of captured ships. Just as the Romans paraded captured generals and troops through the streets of Rome, other victors have exhibited the captured vessels of an enemy. Although there are numerous naval memorials in the United States, the *Arizona* is unique in being the nation's only major naval memorial vessel associated with disaster. Although the destruction of the USS *Maine* propelled the nation into war against Spain in 1898, only pieces are displayed. Other sunken warships lie unmarked in the ocean, with plaques ashore, commemorating their memory, crews, and loss. The *Arizona* serves as a naval memorial in large part because of its accessibility. Admiral Kidd, Jr. noted that the battleship is the only warship lost during World War II whose wreckage still remained in sight when the war was over; all the others went down in deep water and "their bones rest in unknown lands beneath the sea." The *Utah* also remained in sight at war's end, but not in the public eye. The *Arizona's* extraordinary sacrifice, its unique national exposure, and its continued visibility after the war made it a unique naval memorial.

The *Arizona* as a War Memorial

As early as during the war, the U.S. Navy discussed plans to make the ship's visible remains a war memorial. Even then, divergent views on a memorial's nature and purpose reflected the mythic quality of the ship and its symbolism. While ultimately the ship was to serve as a war grave, it was the primary interest of the U.S. Navy to memorialize the ship as a "Navy obligation to what had been one of the fleet's proudest ships and the sailors who went down with her." The ship itself, while a naval memorial and war grave, is not the war memorial. That distinction belongs to the concrete arched structure that spans the sunken hulk but—symbolically—does not touch it. The sunken ship is the artifact and reminder of December 7, 1941. As such, it is a potent symbol that is enhanced and interpreted by the memorial structure. The 1962 memorial, supposedly dipping in the middle to symbolize the initial low point of U.S. fortunes after the attack and rising at both ends to symbolize the nation's rise to victory, is less a memorial to the *Arizona* than it is to the great experience of America in World War II. The *Arizona's* loss serves as a vehicle for personal reflection on the causes, conduct, and results of war. When the shock and initial anger of December 7 had diminished, the *Arizona* transmuted to a symbol of what could happen if the nation were again caught unaware. The battleship stood for the need for military preparedness, for not underestimating potential foes, for alertness, and for mutual understanding and respect.

Archaeological and Anthropological Values

If the remains of Pearl Harbor dead are sacrosanct, the physical remains of ships and aircraft are not. Artifacts salvaged from the *Arizona* are scattered around the United States like holy relics. The ship's formal silver set resides in *Arizona's* state capitol, while one of the ship's bells rests in the visitor center ashore. An anchor from the ship adorns the entrance. Fragments and instruments from Japanese planes shot down during the attack are displayed at Pearl Harbor and elsewhere in the United States. The maps and drawings of the *Arizona* impart a fuller sense of what lies beneath the oil-soaked waters of the harbor, and are eagerly sought. Similarly, the scale model of the wreck intrigues visitors who seek more than glimpses from the memorial.

The Symbolic Value of the *Arizona*

The remains of the *Arizona* are the major focal point for visitors to Pearl Harbor. There has been some discussion of whether interest in World War II sites will diminish when the last of the combatants is gone. Such was not the case with the Civil War, as attested by a host of sites, museums, and books. The interest in the *Arizona* might decline in future generations, but the basic purpose of the memorial and its dependence on the ship probably make that unlikely. As a naval memorial, the *Arizona* will always be the subject of honor and reflection by the U.S. Navy. To other Americans, the ship and its memorial will continue to be a major American shrine, for it reflects the basic truths of how we perceive and deal with war. It remains a potent symbol, meaning many things to many people. For those survivors of the event, and for the families of those dead entombed in the ship, the *Arizona* is a place to come to confront the past and perhaps come to terms with it.

For many Americans the *Arizona* symbolizes the character of the enemy attack. While the Japanese were castigated for a "suicide" mentality during the war, particularly for Kamikaze plane attacks, Americans also honored the same ideal. Historian John W. Dower notes that, "On the eve of Pearl Harbor, one of Hollywood's most popular offerings was 'They Died with Their Boots On', an Errol Flynn movie commemorating Custer's Last Stand." For some, then, the *Arizona* is a symbol speaking to those values, much like Custer's battlefield or the Alamo. The issue of Japanese "infamy" and "perfidy" will probably ultimately fade, but the universal concept of sacrifice and honor of those who died for an ideal will not. The ultimate symbolism of the *Arizona* and the memorial, however, is the basic perception of war and its conduct. To many Americans of an older generation, the *Arizona*, the national symbol of the Japanese attack on Pearl Harbor, also symbolizes the need for preparedness, for military strength, and for alertness.

To a later generation that fought in Vietnam or protested against that war, the *Arizona* has been seen as a memorial to the futility of war and the inevitability and finality of death brought by the use of force between nations. Whatever the perception, however, the *Arizona* is a symbol, and the ultimate significance of the vessel and its memorial lies in the ability to be all things to all people. The *Arizona* and the events of December 7, 1941 continue to reflect cherished stories and cultural values and beliefs, not only of Americans but also of people from other lands and cultures as they also confront the face of war.

Dr. James P. Delgado is the executive director of the Institute of Nautical Archaeology and the adjunct professor of archaeology at Simon Fraser University. He has served as the head of the NPS Maritime Preservation Program, the executive director of the Vancouver Maritime Museum and host of National Geographic Television's "The Sea Hunters." Author or editor of more than thirty books, he authored the National Historic Landmark studies for the wrecks of Pearl Harbor and has dived on the *Arizona*.

A FINAL TOAST AND HONOR

A final toast to their former shipmates. From left to right: Lauren Bruner, John Anderson, Louis Conter, and Donald Stratton.

[All images by Brett Seymour, NPS SRC]

On the afternoon of December 7, 2014, during the 73rd anniversary of the sinking of their ship, four of the nine remaining *Arizona* survivors of the Pearl Harbor attack—John Anderson, Lauren Bruner, Louis Conter, and Donald Stratton—visited the USS *Arizona* Memorial for their final reunion. This event marked the end of a tradition for the survivors who have announced that this was their final official gathering. While at the memorial, the four former shipmates poured a "final toast" to their comrades who had been killed during the attack on Pearl Harbor

or who had deceased in the years since. They shared a bottle of wine—a gift from President Gerald R. Ford to the USS *Arizona* Reunion Association in 1975—drinking from original champagne glasses from the *Arizona*. According to the four survivors, this final salute symbolized the brotherhood and sacrifice of the day of the attack on Pearl Harbor 73 years ago.

After the toast ceremony, the survivors handed one of the glasses to a team of U.S. Navy and National Park Service divers who placed it at the base of the *Arizona's* gun turret No. 4 which also serves as the fi-

nal resting place for survivors of the attack who wish to have their ashes placed on board their former ship.

Louis Conter shared his feelings on the event: "It was amazing for the four of us. I think we all felt

One of the glasses rests on turret No. 4 before being interred in the *Arizona*.

the same, an honor to toast the 1,177 shipmates that we had and who died that day. And the glass which is now interred there [at gun turret No. 4], will give us a chance to have something to drink out of when we're buried there." Despite the official announcement that this event was the last official gathering at the USS *Arizona* Memorial, the men still plan to get together—regardless of the location. "I don't think this is going to be our last [meeting]," said Louis Conter. "We still have time to go, so I think we'll be back out here no matter whether the rest of the crowd can make it or not."

Interments of USS *Arizona* Survivors

Over the years, many Pearl Harbor survivors have been returning to Hawaii to pay their respects to their fallen shipmates, most who were in their early 20s when their lives were taken from them. Many survivors lost their friends, brothers, sons, or fathers on December 7, 1941. A total of 334 crew members survived the sinking of the *Arizona*. Some of them have one last wish—to be interred with their fallen shipmates upon their death. Survivors who assigned to the ship on that fateful day can be interred on the *Arizona*. Pearl Harbor survivors can have their ashes scattered over the waters of Pearl Harbor. The memorial service and interment of deceased *Arizona* survivors is conducted on the USS *Arizona* Memorial. The ceremony includes a committal service, the interment, a rifle salute, TAPS, as well as a flag and plaque presentation. More than forty survivors haven chosen to be interred along with their former shipmates. Glenn H. Lane found his final resting place on board his ship in 2012, followed by Edward L. Wentzlaff in 2013 and John D. Anderson in 2016.

The urns containing the remains of John Anderson and Clarendon R. Hetrick await interment at the memorial.
[Nardel Gervacio, U.S. Navy]

A sailor presents the American flag to the family of John Anderson.
[Somers Steelman, U.S. Navy]

Divers take John Anderson's ashes to their final resting place at *Arizona's* gun turret No. 4, thus reuniting John with his twin brother Delbert who died on board on December 7, 1941.

[All photos by Brett Seymour, NPS SRC - except where noted]

Honoring a Hero

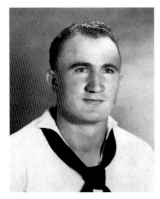

Joe George saved the lives of six *Arizona* crew members.
[NPS]

Following the massive explosion that sank the *Arizona*, six crew members were trapped in her portside control tower on the main mast, kept there by the fires raging below. Already badly burned, they tried to escape the ship. Joe George, a petty officer first class on board the repair ship USS *Vestal* spotted them and threw them a line, in spite of being ordered to cut the line between the *Vestal* and the sinking *Arizona*. Climbing hand over hand across the rope, all six sailors made it across alive—among them were Donald Stratton and Lauren Bruner. Joe George who passed away in 1996, was never officially recognized for saving six lives. Eventually, on December 7, 2017, Rear Admiral Matthew J. Carter, deputy commander of the U.S. Pacific Fleet, presented the Bronze Star Medal with "V" Device for valor for Joseph "Joe" L. George to George's daughter, Joe Ann Taylor, on board the USS *Arizona* Memorial. Donald Stratton and Lauren Bruner had petitioned for this honorable award for many years and attended the ceremony.

We all made it across the line because of the bravery of the seaman, Joe George. Two men died of their burns that day at the hospital and the four other men, Bruner, Lott, Rhiner, and myself lived. I was in the hospital for a year, but because of Joe George went on to have a family. There are two of us alive today. Joe George was never awarded anything for his bravery and going against a direct order from his captain who wanted to pull away from the Arizona and leave us all to die.
—Donald Stratton

The six of us would not have survived except for his courage, in spite of being at high risk himself. He fully deserves high commendations for his actions.
—Lauren Bruner

Historian Daniel Martinez shows Joe Ann Taylor a photo of her father.

Joe Ann Taylor with *Arizona* survivors Donald Stratton and Lauren Bruner who helped to make this award possible.

There is no greater company that I'd rather keep,
than those resting in waters beneath my feet.

Below is a castle of steel that was their home.
Bodies long gone yet their souls still roam.

Their names etched in marble on a memorial that straddles her sides,
while at main and center mast her country's flag still flies.

Many walk hallowed grounds in footsteps of heroes fallen in the past,
I swam with them in a moment frozen in time that was their last.

Solemn homage is paid by those who have lived,
and to rejoin their brothers, their ashes they would give.

Those who survived who have chosen to return,
now lie in eternity in their ship, a collective urn.

Some see only death and destruction
where there is beauty and perfection.

So few were honored as I,
to descend to where the beauty lie.

Mourn not for those who sacrificed and were a loss,
simply thank them in eternity when your path will cross.

By Joey Hutton